Forty Buildings

This book was published in 2009 to celebrate the 40th anniversary of the Hackney Society. At the time the Chair, Kevin Moore, noted that it was the first book to be published in ten years by the Society. Such was the quality of the contributions from the forty authors, combined with the splendid photographs, that it has proved a great success. The hard work put into the ambitious project by Lisa Rigg, as editor, and Glory Hall, as designer, has paid off handsomely.

When the Society decided to undertake a reprint, we were faced with a dilemma. So much has happened in the borough in the intervening years. The decision to locate the Olympic Park in Hackney has seen the erection of many new buildings, some ephemeral, some here to stay. The infrastructure has been updated, and in particular, the railway system has been brought into the 20th, let alone the 21st century.

All this means that many of the comments about the social context in which the 40 buildings were contained are out of date. Also the situation of some of these buildings has changed in the past four years. Haggerston School for Girls and Mossbourne Academy have both gained extensions. Buyers have been found for Pond House and the New Lansdowne Club but the future of Haggerston Baths remains precarious. Cleeve Workshops have been refurbished but Space Studios have gone.

Rewriting and redesigning the book would not only be financially unviable, but also spoil its integrity. The Society has therefore decided to retain the text as it stood in 2009, correcting the few errors or typos that have been noted. In exceptional circumstances, an editorial note for 2013 has been added. Thus we are providing a snapshot of the architecture of Hackney as the borough prepared itself to be one of the hosts of the London 2012 Olympics.

We must once more thank all those who contributed so generously to the project: authors, photographers, editors and our designer. The book stands as a tribute to how special is the architecture of this fascinating part of London. And, as Kevin pointed out in his note, you can help by joining the Hackney Society.

Margaret Willes, 2013

Hackney
Modern, Restored, Forgotten, Ignored

40 Buildings to mark 40 Years

of the Hackney Society

Edited by Lisa Rigg

Hackney Society

First published in 2009
by The Hackney Society
The Round Chapel
1d Glenarm Road
London E5 0LY

Reprint 2013

E: info@hackneysociety.org
www.hackneysociety.org

ISBN: 978-0-9536734-1-4

Typeset in Myriad
Designed by Design@GloryHall.com

Generously funded by Awards for All (England).

The Hackney Society works to preserve Hackney's unique heritage
and make the area a better place in which to live and work.
Formed in 1967 it seeks to involve and support local people in the
regeneration and conservation of Hackney's built environment
and open spaces. We aim to promote high standards of planning,
architecture and conservation in Hackney; give a voice to local
people in the future development of the borough; and educate
and foster public interest in the history, architecture and
character of Hackney.

The Society meets monthly for a programme of walks, tours and talks
about Hackney's modern and historic buildings; publishes books,
newsletters and walks on that subject; organises special community
projects; and comments on planning applications.

The Hackney Society is a membership organisation and is a
registered charitable company. An elected board of trustees, drawn
from the membership, manages the work of the Society. The Hackney
Society is a civic and amenity society.

In memory of David Batchelder
Born 21 March 1939; died 6 June 2008

Chair of the Hackney Society from 1974 to the 1980s

For Solomon – LR

Contents

Foreword   11
Acknowledgements   12
Introduction   13

Modern – post-1960 buildings   **16**
1.   Adelaide Wharf *Lisa Rigg*   18
2.   Doris's Place *Tom Dyckhoff*   22
3.   Geffrye Museum Extension *David Heath*   25
4.   Haggerston School for Girls *Anthony Thistleton*   28
5.   Hothouse *Tim Ronalds*   32
6.   In-Between *Tim Horsey*   35
7.   Mossbourne Community Academy *Geraldine Bedell*   38
8.   Rivington Place *Amin Taha*   41
9.   Rowe Lane *Cathy Strongman*   44
10. Truman's Road *Kevin Moore*   47

Restored – historic buildings that have been saved   **50**
11. 91-101 Worship Street *Chris Miele*   52
12. The Castle Climbing Centre *Allen Abramson*   55
13. Clapton Portico Learning Centre *Vyki Sparkes*   59
14. Hackney Empire *Patrick Lynch*   62
15. London Fields Lido *Margaret Willes*   66
16. The Round Chapel *Laurie Elks*   69
17. St Augustine's Tower *Nick Holder*   72
18. Shoreditch Town Hall *Joanna Smith*   75
19. Stoke Newington West Reservoir Centre *Monica Blake*   78
20. Sutton House *Paul Bolding*   81

Forgotten – lost buildings   **84**
21. Atlas Works *Patrick Hammill*   86
22. Bishopsgate Station and Goods Yard *Jerry Tate*   89
23. Clapton Federation Synagogue *Sharman Kadish*   92
24. Eton Manor Boys' Club *Ann Robey*   96
25. Hackney Stadium *Matt Payne*   100
26. The Mothers' Hospital *Ken Worpole*   103
27. Nichols Square *Ann Robey*   106
28. Pitfield Street Baths and Washhouses *Heloise Brown*   110
29. Trowbridge Estate *Chris Dorley-Brown*   114
30. Woodberry Down Comprehensive School *Ray Rogers*   117

Ignored – in need of some love and attention   **120**
31. Abney Park Chapel *David Solman*   122
32. Cleeve Workshops *Sarah Wise*   125
33. Haggerston Baths *John O'Callaghan and the Haggerston Baths Community trust* 128
34. New Lansdowne Club *Isobel Watson*   131
35. Nicholl House *Suzanne Waters*   134
36. Palace Pavilion *Julia Lafferty and Patrick Vernon*   137
37. Pond House *Amy Erickson*   141
38. St Mary of Eton Church *Elizabeth Robinson*   145
39. Sight of Eternal Life Church *David Solman*   148
40. Space Studios *John Turner*   151

Appendix I - IV   154
Endnotes   158
Contributors   159
Selected bibliography and sources   163
Photo credits   166
Index   167

Foreword

The best perspective to be had on the rich disorder of Hackney's townscape and architecture is from the train travelling from Stamford Hill to Cambridge Heath, and back again. For most of the journey passengers are transported, as if by magic carpet, above the rooftops of an astonishing assembly of old manorial estates, parks, cemeteries, roads, canals, branch railways, medieval churches, almshouses, synagogues, mosques, Georgian terraces, tower blocks, bath-houses, hospitals, asylums, libraries, museums, charitable settlements, factories, workshops, breaker's yards, pubs, clubs, street markets, shops, cinemas and theatres – and much else. One lifetime alone is not long enough to make sense of it all.

All human life is here, as is much of the area's history of the past five hundred years. The borough has been by turns manorial and pastoral, High Church and Tory, Gothic and romantic, industrial and penitential, radical and reforming, as well as a laboratory for Functionalist command planning. More recently it has become a relatively successful exercise in cosmopolitan live and let live. All of these layers of social history are reflected in the buildings which make up Hackney, and which this collection of essays properly commemorates. Gratitude is due to Lisa Rigg and her colleagues at the Hackney Society for bringing the project to fruition.

What is particularly striking is that so many of these buildings were conceived and executed in the belief that a better life was there to be had by many, if not all. Few expressed it quite as directly as the prospectus of the Eton Mission, cited by Elizabeth Robinson, which was 'to help the people of Hackney Wick to Heaven'. My Jewish father-in-law, a keen member of the Eton Manor Boys' Club, would certainly have resisted this entreaty. Nevertheless whether it was in the provision of places of worship described here (The Round Chapel, Clapton Federation Synagogue, Sight of Eternal Life Church), of education (Haggerston School for Girls, Mossbourne Community Academy), of the cultivation of the healthy body (Pitfield Street Baths and Washhouses, Haggerston Baths, London Fields Lido), of political endeavour (Shoreditch Town Hall with its motto: *'More Light, More Power'*) or of entertainment (Hackney Empire, Palace Pavilion), the drive to collective improvement as well as individual self-fulfilment remains a leitmotif of Hackney life, and its vari-coloured jigsaw of buildings and inter-locking neighbourhoods and historic villages.

There is another area in which the borough's building stock seems purpose-built for its economic destiny, often inscribed in the original design. This was the notion of 'live-work', both as an architectural intention but also as a social ideal. Chris Miele's account of 91-101 Worship Street, describes an exquisite terrace of artisan workshops and accommodation designed by Philip Webb, a close friend and devotee of William Morris, still in use. Elsewhere Sarah Wise recalls the fascinating history of Cleeve Workshops, part of what had been intended as a 'working village' on the pioneering Boundary Estate. In recent times this wish to integrate living and working is reflected in Adelaide Wharf, where offices and housing are established on the same site, and at Doris's Place where, according to Tom Dyckhoff, 'two flats, a work space and a gallery/shop space [are] all tightly organised round a central courtyard'. Add to this the often ingenious refurbishments to historic terrace houses or infill developments by inventive architectural practices, and this demonstrates that whatever exists in Hackney can nearly always be adapted or improved rather than simply knocked down. There will always be room for the new here as well.

There is one building type in which Hackney is particularly well endowed – though it gains only one entry here – and that is the railway station. The borough has upwards of ten, used by thousands of residents and visitors daily. In quality they range from the poor to the appalling. While vision, hard work and money have gone into refurbishing much of Hackney's historic buildings, its railway heritage remains in serious disrepair, even though growing environmental concerns and transport initiatives may result in it being required to play a greater role in Hackney's future.

Though this and a number of other lessons can be taken from the essays which follow, the most forceful is a realisation that buildings work best when they are informed by a vision of the greater scheme of things. The case study buildings described here were mostly envisaged, funded, designed and built by separate hands, and certainly according to a wide range of belief systems and political impulses: nevertheless they worked cumulatively and collectively to produce today's Hackney, still imbued with traces of those original social and religious ideals. The urban historian Jane Jacobs once wrote that, "Old ideas can sometimes use new buildings, (while) new ideas must come from old buildings." This paradox reminds us that though Hackney retains a reputation for being socially and architecturally contrarian, it remains a highly creative and distinctive corner of the world, possibly without equal.

Ken Worpole, September 2009

Acknowledgements

The idea for this book began with a discussion with Rossana Tich, a trustee, who wanted to produce a publication to mark the Hackney Society's 40th anniversary. This led to fundraising for a small grant from Awards for All – a Lottery fund distributor, and Hackney Parochial Charities. The condition of the Awards for All grant being that we involve the community and encourage voluntary contribution, which as you can see from the long acknowledgments has been achieved beyond all expectation. The buildings were nominated by the general public and short-listed by an advisory committee. The contributing authors selected a building to research from a short-list of 50.

This book could have not have been published without the generosity of Awards for All, and the dedication and enthusiasm of the many people who contributed to it. A special thanks to the following people and organisations who generously donated time, words and photographs.

Words: Allen Abramson, Geraldine Bedell, Monica Blake, Paul Bolding, Heloise Brown, Chris Dorley-Brown, Tom Dyckhoff, Laurie Elks, Amy Erickson, Haggerston Pool Community Trust, Patrick Hammill, David Heath, Nick Holder, Tim Horsey, Sharman Kadish, Julia Lafferty, Patrick Lynch, Chris Miele, Kevin Moore, John O'Callaghan, Matt Payne, Ann Robey, Elizabeth Robinson, Ray Rogers, Tim Ronalds, Joanna Smith, David Solman, Cathy Strongman, Vyki Sparkes, Amin Taha, Jerry Tate, Anthony Thistleton, John Turner, Patrick Vernon, Suzanne Waters, Isobel Watson, Margaret Willes, Sarah Wise and Ken Worpole.

Photographs: Alan Baxter and Associates, Peter Barber Architects, Brady Mallalieu Architects, Heloise Brown, Rob Barton, David Churchill, Inge Clemente, Nigel Corrie, Dominic Cullinan, Chris Dorley-Brown, Martin Dusashenka, Stephen Gill, Masood Golsorkhi, Tim Grose, Nick Guttridge, Nick Holder, Nicholas Kane, Katsu Kida, Kevin Lake, Julian Mason, Jane Parker, Hedy Pary-Davies, Played in Britain, Ed Reeve, S&P Architects, Grant Smith, Shoreditch Town Hall Trust, Tim Soar, David Solman and Gesche Wuerfel.

Also, I would like to thank following individuals for their help and assistance: Jo Adams, Libby Adams, Admiral Ken, John Allan, David Alsford, Cany Ash, Siân Batchelder, Sheila Benjamin, Gary Butler, Stephen Coley, Audrey Destandau, David Dewing, Irvine Douglas, Tony Dyson, Kate Emmerson, Sally England, Mavis Gaza, Sophia Gibb, Tony Gillett, Elizabeth Green, Gemma Hall, Ivan Harbour, Simon Inglis, Will Johnson, Marcus Lee, Will Lee, Eleanor Lowenthal, Monika Kowalczyk, Kate Ledwith, Siân Mogridge, Cindy Molenaar, Negin Moghaddam, Jan Pimblett, John Potter, Maureen Roberts, Annabel Rootes, Robert Sakula, Mark Samuel, Tom Schollar, Stuart Sloan, Robin Sorrell, Michael Taylor, Rossana Tich, June Warrington, Barbara Wheeler-Early, Sieta Whitehead, Laura Whitton, Nigel Wilkins and Mandy Williams.

I would like to say a special thank you to the advisory committee who helped me to short-list the buildings: Amin Taha, Tom Dyckhoff, Victor Belcher, Kevin Moore and Mick Ferris. I would also like to say a big thank you to: David Heath, Tim Horsey, Helen King, Natasha Lewer, Ann Robey, Joanna Smith, Isobel Watson and Margaret Willes who helped to proof the copy; Inge Clemente who came to my rescue by taking many of the photographs in this book. She also helped with picture research and corrected the photographs so they were ready for print. I am also very grateful to the editorial advice, patience and kind words given by Nick Holder, Helen King, Ann Robey and Isobel Watson.

I am also particularly indebted to Glory Hall who designed the book and turned my idea into a wonderful reality. Without her patience and dedication this book would never have been realised. She also treated me to the most wonderful home-made cakes while proofing copy. I would also like to express my gratitude and thanks to Ken Worpole. He generously wrote the foreword, edited five contributions, commented on the final draft, and gave me the final bit of encouragement that was needed to finish this immense task.

And finally, I would like to thank the people who drew me to Hackney and then made it difficult to leave: Dan Cope-Stephens, Russell Beck, Emma O'Grady, Caragh Thuring, Natasha Wolffe, and my partner Allen Abramson and son Solomon.

Lisa Rigg

Introduction

By the time I arrived, Hackney was unrecognisable to many of its older inhabitants who remembered the borough as one of industry with the household names of Clarnico, Pilkington, Latham's, Lesney and Berger Paints still fresh in their minds. In 1967, when the Hackney Society was founded by a small group of concerned residents, Hackney, like other East London boroughs, was in the grip of industrial decline. This would lead to the eventual loss or reuse of many buildings – with warehouses, factories, gas plants, power stations, tram depots and timber wharves either demolished or left derelict. During the 1970s and 1980s a surplus of these buildings allowed creative industries to flourish. Photographers, printers, musicians, artists, filmmakers, designers and prop-makers came to live and work in the borough, creating the distinctive sub-culture that still exists today. But, unlike then, Hackney now suffers from a lack of affordable light industrial units, making small-scale manufacturing virtually impossible, and forcing some creative enterprises to relocate to cheaper areas.

In 1986 the Society published a book based on a survey of industrial buildings in south Shoreditch and concurrently undertook a survey of industrial archaeology in Hackney Wick, which was never published. Paradoxically, finding itself located on the edge of the site of the 2012 Olympic Games, Hackney Wick is now teetering on the verge of redevelopment. The tower blocks, which replaced the Victorian two-up, two-downs, that originally housed factory workers have gone, and the few remaining warehouses, wharves and factories are hanging on for dear life. Sadly, the history and legacy of this area is on the verge of annihilation, and unlike Shoreditch, will not bask in the splendour of the many restored industrial buildings that remain there.

This slow and stealthy erosion of historic Hackney was one of the reasons why Michael Thomas, Sir John Betjeman, Jack Youngmark, David Batchelder, Israel Renson, Irene Chaplin and others formed the Hackney Society. They wanted to protect what was historically significant, beautiful and ultimately irreplaceable. Due to war, social upheaval, shifts in population and poverty, Hackney's 18th- and 19th-century streetscapes were in ruins, with bomb-damaged buildings in many parts of the borough, particularly Haggerston and Hoxton.

In the earlier days of the Society there were a number of campaigns worthy of support. In the 1960s, Hackney Council's housing and transport policy envisaged the redevelopment of 95 per cent of the borough. Like other civic and amenity societies, the Society grew out of the growing concern among its residents for what planners and architects saw as the solution to the post-war housing crisis and decades of neglect. For example, the newly formed London Borough of Hackney wanted to demolish most of Mapledene Road and replace it with tower blocks. This led to the Mapledene Public Inquiry in 1971-2 and an early victory for the Society. Other contentious proposals included the development of the 'East Cross Route,' 'North Cross Route' and 'Eastern Avenue Extension' motorways that, if built, would have resulted in the loss of the Eton Manor Boys' Club (see Ann Robey, page 96), Victoria Park and part of the Regent's Canal. Luckily, only the 'East Cross Route' was built, with the other two proposals being left on the drawing board.

Above: Carless, Capel and Leonard, Hackney Wick.

At this time an official memo was posted in the planning department forbidding any planning officer from speaking to any member of the Hackney Society. In the early days, as well as being effective agitators, the Society also germinated many ideas that Hackney Council have since adopted as their own. In 1967 the Society ran an 'I Love Hackney' poster campaign and developed a series of walks in five areas that later were designated conservation areas. In 1970 the Hackney Society Design Awards were initiated. Since then, the Society has built bridges with the Council and achieved in partnership many positive initiatives and outcomes: surveys of listed buildings and 'Buildings at Risk'; Conservation Areas Advisory Committees; and it has become the official community consultee to the Council on planning matters.

In 1979, the Society's first book *From Tower To Tower Block: the Buildings of Hackney* was published. Written jointly by six members, it opened with the statement that "of all the buildings in Britain those in Hackney must be among the most unloved". Despite being a later arrival in the borough, I can remember the remnants of this era. Victorian terraces on Dalston Lane (opposite the Pembury Estate) stood unoccupied and derelict; squatters in London Lane and Ellingfort Road fought the Council to save more Victorian houses from demolition; the Hackney Empire had become a gaudy reincarnation of its former glory in desperate need of restoration and up-to-date technical facilities; King's Hall, Haggerston Baths and Britannia Leisure Centre were the only swimming pools, with London Fields Lido full of buddleia rather than water.

Above: Berger Paint Factory, Morning Lane.

Ironically, being "unloved" contributed to saving many historic buildings in the borough. In 1991, the first year of English Heritage's national 'Buildings at Risk' register, Hackney had a phenomenal 101 entries (compared to 32 in 2009). Hoxton Hall, which has been on the register since its inception, has at last been removed. Since 1967, 472 structures have been statutorily listed, with only a handful de-listed. This has also contributed to protecting 18th-19th- and 20th-century architecture in the borough.

In the mid-1990s regeneration money and the Heritage Lottery Fund became the panacea for decades of neglect and under-investment in the built environment. Around £22 million has been awarded by the Heritage Lottery Fund to building and restoration projects in Hackney, in stark contrast to just £2.8 million from English Heritage. £16 million of this has been allocated to the restoration of historic buildings and open spaces – with the largest grants awarded to the Hackney Empire (£4.58 million) and Clissold Park (£4.46 million). Only £2.82 million has been given to religious buildings, as the Heritage Lottery Fund does not tend to fund religious groups. This perhaps reflects why churches and cemeteries currently make up 28 per cent of entries on the 2009 'Buildings at Risk' register. (See Appendix II for a list of grants awarded).

Sir John Betjeman, co-founder of The Victorian Society, who wrote the foreword to *From Tower to Tower Block*, stated: "It is natural that this never-fashionable London district should breed great characters and much kindness." While the latter may still be true, in 2009 Hackney is possibly a victim of its own success. Hoxton, Shoreditch and Broadway Market are now visitor destinations, and indeed fashionable places to live. Back in 1995, when I first arrived in Hackney, I wouldn't have predicted being able to buy a freshly ground cup of coffee in many of these neighbourhoods, let alone enjoy the delis, restaurants, bars and art galleries that now populate them.

The downside of this increase in popularity has been unprecedented levels of development, with a planning department seemingly overwhelmed with the volume of planning applications. So, while many buildings have been restored, reused and saved, the inertia of the 1970s and 1980s no longer exists to help protect the historic fabric of Hackney. People do want to live here, despite being ranked as one of the most deprived local authorities in England. Moreover, poverty is visibly polarised, with pockets of extreme deprivation directly next door to £1million homes.

The borough's once lamentable public realm and public services, something that Elizabeth Robinson identified as "Hackney's abiding problem" in the Society's last publication *Twentieth Century Buildings in Hackney* (1999) – have more or less been remedied in the short-term. Currently, residents can enjoy nine open spaces with 'green flag' status; proximity to central London with improved cycle routes and public transport; street and farmers' markets in Stoke Newington and Broadway Market; new sports and library facilities (see Allen Abramson, page 55; Margaret Willes, page 66; Monica Blake, page 78); new education facilities (see Geraldine Bedell, page 38; Vyki Sparkes, page 59); and a thriving arts and cultural scene (see Tim Ronalds, page 32; Patrick Lynch, page 62).

In the last ten years, Hackney has seen a renaissance in high-rise and high-density development. This to the casual observer may seem perverse after a period which saw the demolition of some 23 tower blocks in 18 years, starting with the demolition of Northaird Point in 1985 (see Chris Dorley-Brown, page 114). Today the skyline is once again being punctuated by ten to 19-storey housing developments. Much of this is due to the intensification of housing provision as set out in *The London Plan: Spatial Development Strategy for Greater London* (2004). Over a 20-year period (1997-2016) Hackney needs to create 14,310 new homes, 715 homes a year. In comparison to other inner-London boroughs this is relatively low – Southwark needs 29,530 and Islington 18,070 new homes – but still an appreciable target to reach, and one which threatens the historic environment of Hackney. *The London Plan* and Hackney Council's 'un-adopted' *Tall Buildings Strategy* (2005) sets out opportunity areas for development – Shoreditch, the Lower Lea Valley, London Fields and Dalston being areas where the Society needs to stay vigilant. Unfortunately, the London Borough of Hackney could be on the brink of re-creating the high-rise slums of the past.

Above: War-damaged buildings in Cleveleys Road, c.1942.

Another threat to the historic environment comes in the form of climate change and the uncertainties inherent in future climate projections. In 2009 most of us are aware that as individuals we need to reduce our carbon footprint, but are badly informed about the best way to do this. In the UK, 46 per cent of carbon emissions can be attributed to the energy requirements of buildings, with approximately half of this total from homes. Upgrading the energy efficiency of traditional buildings has an important role to play in meeting targets for reducing emissions. In the near future owners of these buildings will need

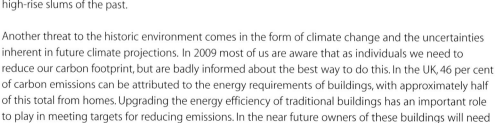

to consider how to adapt their homes to become more energy efficient, hopefully without destroying the historic character of the buildings. English Heritage warns that it is "incorrect to assume that the older a building is the less energy efficient it is". They are also "concerned that poorly founded assumptions that modern buildings inevitably out-perform older ones could result in proposals to demolish housing stock to make way for new-build". This is a real threat to many older buildings in Hackney – not just 18th- and 19th-century buildings, but also scores of post-war housing. The sustainability debate could result in perfectly 'adaptable' buildings being "threatened by poorly designed adaptation responses", or demolished. In Hackney, many wooden and metal window frames have been replaced with uPVC due to a misguided perception that they require no maintenance and increase energy savings. This has had an adverse effect on many conservation areas and listed buildings. By contrast, suitably managed, high-performance timber windows with a micro-porous water-based paint can provide a life-long solution.

This book sets out to commemorate the 40th anniversary of the Hackney Society, which took place in 2007. The inspiration came from the series of wonderful books that the Society published in the 20-year period between 1979 and 1999. Some of these, which are now sadly out of print, tell the story of the development of Hackney and its buildings and have been invaluable in the production of this book. *Hackney – Modern, Restored, Forgotten, Ignored* sets out to draw attention to good-quality modern architecture that has been built since 1960; recent restoration projects; buildings that have been lost since 1960; and buildings that are currently at risk from neglect or demolition. To choose just 40 buildings was very difficult, so understandably many buildings of note have not been included: Hoxton Hall, Sanford Terrace, Hackney Pavilion, the Rio Cinema, The Circus Space, St Leonard's Church, Dalston Theatre, Clapton Stadium, 187 and 191 Stoke Newington High Street, St Mary's Lodge, Hackney and East London Synagogue, St Columba's Church, Nile Street and the Shoreditch Prototype House, to name just a few.

Each chapter focuses on ten buildings and aims to provide a varied selection of typologies, periods and geographic locations, chosen so as not to duplicate too many of the buildings featured in previous publications. Buildings such as Northaird Point on the Trowbridge Estate and Hackney Stadium were proposed due to their social and historical significance rather than for their architecture, which particularly in the case of Northaird Point would be hard to defend. But no book about Hackney would be complete without a mention of these icons of the 20th century. Woodberry Down Comprehensive School, demolished as it was being considered for listing, was also a fine example of post-war design (see Ray Rogers, page 117). Other buildings like Nicholl House (see Suzanne Waters, page 134), and the Palace Pavilion (see Julia Lafferty and Patrick Vernon, page 137), while not worthy of listing, should be recognised and valued for their local architectural and historic importance, and if possible be refurbished and saved.

Above: Georgian terrace being restored, Stoke Newington Church Street.

In the year that saw the shocking and sudden demise of the Civic Trust – the charity that represented civic and amenity societies across England (to which the Hackney Society was affiliated) – the Society shares a similarly uncertain future. In the last few years funding has been hard to secure, only one part-time worker has been employed, and more people may prefer to start their own independent campaigns rather than joining a seemingly more cumbersome and 'traditional' organisation. This trend seems to be widespread, but after a period of near collapse the Society is beginning to see some 'green shoots' of recovery – membership is increasing, its books are back in local shops, and a thriving programme of events is currently being enjoyed by members and non-members alike. A number of National Lottery-funded projects, including this publication and another project, *From Fever to Consumption: the Story of Healthcare in Hackney*, have engaged the skills, expertise and energies of those interested in the history and environment of Hackney and allowed the community to become involved in Hackney-wide projects. The Hackney Society, like Hackney itself, is no longer unloved and marginal but at the centre of a regenerated East End.

As a borough-wide civic and amenity society, the Hackney Society needs to attract the support of its residents and to avoid complacency in relation to its past achievements. Hackney hosts a distinctive configuration of buildings possessing a delicate balance of the old and the new. Architectural fashions change, politicians and planners come and go, and professional memories are short. But Hackney residents are left to live with the long-term consequences of policies that, while cheap and fashionable at the time, may jar with future local need and taste. It is essential that the Society remains vigilant.

Lisa Rigg, August 2009

Above: River Lea and the Lesney factory in the background.

Modern

post-1960 buildings

"Society needs a good image of itself.
That is the job of the architect."

Walter Gropius

Lisa Rigg

Adelaide Wharf

Queensbridge Road E2

Architect Allford Hall Monaghan Morris 2007

As you travel along the towpath of the Regent's Canal – from City Road Basin in Islington to the Cat and Mutton Bridge at Broadway Market – you pass a succession of residential and commercial developments that have started to replace the old canalside industrial buildings. Gone are most of the timber and builders' wharves, gas plants and the associated industrial buildings that once lined this watery corridor. As you approach the elliptical arch of the bridge at Queensbridge Road, across the water is the latest colourful solution to the UK's housing crisis.

Adelaide Wharf, designed by Allford Hall Monaghan Morris, is a sustainable housing development with a hidden social agenda. Contained within its glossy, vitreous enamel-lined entrances, and rough-sawn Siberian larch and smooth zinc façade, are 147 flats and 690 square metres of office space that seek to create a 'genuine mixed community'.

The building consists of three blocks arranged in a U-shape around a landscaped courtyard. The development provides private, social and affordable key worker housing. The size and layout of all the apartments are the same, with similar standards achieved in the internal fixtures and fittings across all tenures. This sets the building apart from many similar developments in Hackney.

The high quality design and decent proportion of 'affordable' key worker homes was made possible by the unique way in which the land was secured. The development, part of English Partnerships' *London-Wide Initiative,* is one of 16 sites in London set aside to provide low-cost home ownership schemes for key workers. English Partnerships, who originally owned the land and commissioned the scheme, took a delayed land payment. The unusual approach gave the developer First Base a number of years, rather than one, to pay for the land. This allowed greater investment in the

Far left: Looking east along Regent's Canal towards the bridge and Adelaide Wharf with its faux lifting cranes.

Above: Main entrance lobby.

design and meant the inclusion of 50 per cent affordable housing – although the price for a 1-bedroom flat required a hefty deposit and a moderately sized annual salary.

Unsurprisingly, the private housing is mainly located on the canalside, as waterside locations increase development values by 20 per cent. The social housing has not been relegated to the roadside however, but is located on the sunny southside, overlooking Haggerston Park with views towards the City. At six storeys this is a modest development and fortunately another two storeys were not added – despite the architect's view that the site could have supported a taller building.

Built on the site of the former Haggerston Basin (which was drained and filled in 1967), Adelaide Wharf fits in well with its surroundings and echoes the scale and form of 19th-century waterfront warehouse buildings – unlike developments that are being built further east along the Lee Navigation. The development takes its name from the former timber wharf that occupied part of the site, which presumably imported Australian hardwoods, hence Adelaide. The building has faux lifting cranes providing an elegant supporting structure for cantilevered balconies that enliven the bland façade. Richard Wood's floor-to-ceiling print of wooden floorboards that decorates the main lobby and stairwell makes reference to the area's industrial past, echoing the canal's long tradition of transporting timber for the furniture trade in south Shoreditch.

Since 1999, with the completion of Murray Grove (the UK's first multi-storey Volumetric modular building designed by Cartwright Pickard) in Hoxton and Raines Court in Stoke Newington (also designed by Allford Hall Monaghan Morris), prefabricated methods of construction have become a symbol of 'modern' and 'economical' housing in Britain. Both of these schemes were commissioned by the Peabody Trust who wanted to demonstrate that this form of construction could be cheap, clean and quick to build, thus helping to meet housing shortages. This building signals a move away from poorly designed 'neo-Georgian' developments that pepper our cities. Adelaide Wharf, unlike its other prefabricated predecessors, offers a more flexible, subtle and attractive solution to creating economical, sustainable and energy-efficient architecture.

Despite claims of being a mixed development, the social housing is contained within its own block with a separate and less stunning entrance lobby – no Lubetkin-inspired staggered staircase to give double-height spaces and increased light penetration. The separation of the social housing limits the possibility of 'genuine' social interactions between owner-occupiers and the tenants who rent. This is explained as being necessary to reduce the number of perceived strangers walking the corridors, providing residents with the feeling of a secure environment. It also allows the housing association, Family Mosaic, to manage its own block. This enforced separation between tenures is somewhat remedied by a shared courtyard. This is a great facility and unlike many housing estates can only be accessed by the people who live there.

Hopefully, Adelaide Wharf will not succumb to the problems encountered by tower blocks and high-density housing elsewhere in Hackney, with structural failures and inappropriate choice of materials expensive maintenance costs for the upkeep of lifts and communal areas. Nor will it face the problems associated with intimidating long corridors and open spaces that attract crime and anti-social behaviour. It is also to be hoped that that the private housing will not just be bought as buy-to-lets by private landlords, thus creating a transitory population rather than a stable neighbourly community.

This innovative development mixes social economics with well-designed and stylish apartments. This is to be applauded and encouraged, especially at a time that is witnessing the revival of high-rise buildings, some of which echo the "slums in the sky" of the 1960s and 1970s. Adelaide Wharf offers a viable high-density alternative and is an important step in the future regeneration of Hackney.

Far left: Suspended balconies on the west façade, looking north along Queensbridge Road.

Left: Main stairwell with Richard Wood's artwork on the walls of the internal staircase.

Tom Dyckhoff

Doris's Place

Broadway Market E8

Architect Peter Barber Architects 1996

Of course we're all modern now. Now Britain's been thoroughly Grand Designed and Ikea-ed up. We all know our larch shingle from our Eames recliner. But you have to step back in time. Back to the dark ages. Back, back to a time before Tate Modern. A time when Britain was being reintroduced, gently, to modernism after a 30-year hiatus. Back to the millennium. I was a roving reporter on the *Guardian's* design pages, dispatched to the front line. We'd heard vague, uncorroborated reports that contemporary architecture had been spotted in a distant land called Hackney. I was sent to investigate.

I remember meeting a nice lady called Maureen on Broadway Market. A Broadway Market very different from its incarnation these days, all organic olive oil and air kisses. Back then Broadway Market was more empty shopfronts and ASBOs. Who would dare build the vanguard of modernism here? "Lovely, isn't it?" Maureen

sighed to me. "An alien come from outer space." Maureen, doing her daily shop, put her bags down and joined me in staring goggle-eyed at this miracle. Sharp-suited modern architecture. Here in London. Here in Hackney. A real, genuine, modern house without a single pitched roof, not one faux-Victorian detail. Instead it has oddly shaped windows, a peculiar arched roof, a local nickname ('the parabola building') and thick, dazzling, white walls straight from the Middle East. "I could see myself in that place," she said, picking up her bags. "One day," she laughed.

The miracle came courtesy of architect Peter Barber. Hackney has long been a refuge of artists, creatives, architects and oddballs. But in the late 1990s, with their traditional haunts in Shoreditch proving increasingly expensive, many began moving eastwards. Land around Broadway Market, Bethnal Green and London Fields was then still cheap. Barber became one of a new generation of

Far left: Internal courtyard with curved roofline and 'oddly' shaped windows.

Above: Light-filled interior of one of the flats.

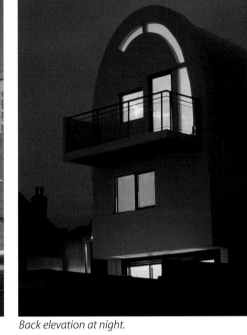

Back elevation.

Back elevation at night.

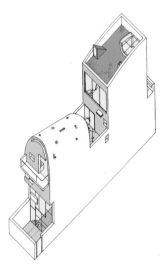

Above: Axonometric drawing of the building.

architects in London beginning to exploit both the gentrification of the East End, and the general cultural shift in Britain in the 1990s, thanks to Ikea, *Wallpaper* Magazine*, the rise of New Labour, towards a resurgence of 'modern style'.

Doris's Place, though, was innovative not just for its style, but for its social agenda. This was an experiment in modern, truly urban living. Two decades after Margaret Thatcher pronounced society dead, here was an architect exploiting the political shift to the left – albeit still within free market economics – to celebrate the collective as well as the private. Doris's, with its neo-Corbusian style and social, almost welfare state agenda, was futuristically nostalgic, an odd mixture indeed. On a postage stamp-sized site Barber squeezed two flats, a work space and a shop/gallery space, all tightly organised round a central courtyard. "I wanted to show that living densely doesn't mean living in a slum," Barber explained at the time. "Instead density is what cities are all about, being able to say hello to your neighbour. In fact, the building's way over the density the council allows. A planning officer looked kindly on us. Yet go inside any one of the units and they're as spacious as a palace, as light-filled as a cathedral. And private. The walls are cut with odd little windows which flash oblique glimpses of your neighbours. But you never look directly onto them – there's neighbourliness, but privacy.

Such experiments weren't then down to any government drive to encourage architecture or big-name developers – that came later – but to that last resort of the British architect: DIY. Barber's development did receive single regeneration

funding, because it invests in the local economy. But the drive behind it came from him and his client – "an extraordinary woman," he says – called Marian Lewis. "I'm a complete architecture junkie," Lewis told me. "I've spent my whole life looking up at buildings. But I'd been longing to start developing, put my money where my taste was." She was lucky to come across Peter (after taking advice from the caff down the road, Peter's local), and Peter was lucky to come across a genuine architectural patron.

Doris's, though, was no high faluting piece of aesthetics. It was grounded in economic reality. Most of the domestic architectural experiments in 1990s London were essentially financed by the decade-long rise in property prices nationally. They exploited the market to snatch what little they could in terms of aesthetic experimentation or social regeneration. Doris's was no exception. Barber's practice, he notes "is committed to the social project of Architecture. We won't change the world. These are small investments in an area which has had its fair share of neglect." He's since gone on to use Doris's template of high-density, socially-minded architecture to create whole, award-winning affordable housing estates in Bow and Barking. "I hope the building is a happy building. I wanted to create a local focal point, something to seduce people inside and out."

Today, as we sit amid the ruins of New Labour's economic vision, it's important to remember the good times as well as the bad – the few moments when a speck of optimism, of faith in society, was grasped. Doris's Place was one such speck of sunshine.

David Heath

Geffrye Museum Extension

Kingsland Road E2

Architect Branson Coates (with Sheppard Robson) 1998

Completed in 1998, the Geffrye Museum extension was recent enough to be included in Elizabeth Robinson's *Twentieth Century Buildings in Hackney* (1999). She wrote that "with the… Extension and the new Clissold Sports Centre, Hackney is seeing out the old century on a high architectural note." These were brave and optimistic words. Looking back from the end of the first decade of the next century we can reflect, yet again, that predicting the future can be a tricky business.

The extension is popular, robust, well detailed, and functioning much as intended. The educational use of the lower floor is thriving. The parts of the design that were admired when it opened still have much to commend them; and the perversity of other parts, such as the rising spiral of the external brickwork which expresses no spiral inside, now seem familiar and quaint, rather than odd and wilful.

For this was and is architecture with an explicit agenda. As Nigel Coates, the architect, wrote: "When visiting the museum, visitors pop out from a timeline of room sets only to discover that the rooms of the twentieth century are not organised as a line but as a loop."

The extension is barely visible from the Kingsland Road side, and it joins the museum at the back in a very clear way – visitors really do pop out from the old building, and no one can fail to understand that they have just left one building period for another. The materials and scale are similar, but they are not the same. And so here there is the respect for context that conservationists always argue is both possible and welcome, but for which they often have difficultly in citing examples. This is no bland contextualism: it is a vigorous modern building, very much of its own time. It is the sort of building where even the most fastidious could still find themselves nodding warm approval of an architect's statement

Above: The Geffrye Museum's new galleries under construction, May 1998.

that he proposed to construct "a diagrid roof… swirled between the brick structures like a cloud."

Looking back, we should be clear that there were concerns as well as praise. The late 1990s was, we now realise, the great period of National Lottery funding. The extension cost £5.3million, of which the Heritage Lottery Fund contributed £3.75million. This was new money on a scale the museum world had not experienced for some time. Those involved were right to be ambitious, but there was a danger that a capital programme creating new heritage would undervalue old heritage where revenue funding was still critical. The external form of the Geffrye Museum had been little altered since it opened as a London County Council museum in 1914. Was the lottery going to mean that monster new extensions were going to crop up everywhere, and that old buildings themselves were still not going to be properly looked after?

But, as it has turned out, the Geffrye Museum extension wasn't the beginning; it was near the end. And it wasn't just the end of this sort of lottery funding. To the surprise of many (or perhaps to their secret relief), Branson Coates, the architects, haven't really built anything else since. There was the (now gone) BodyZone inside the Millennium Dome, the now closed National Centre for Popular Music (Sheffield, 1999) and that has been it. It isn't entirely clear why. In 2008, Nigel Coates was quoted as stating "I didn't go. I just chose to…detach myself for a while."

So what seemed to set a precedent set none, or very little. We can now look at the magnificent central staircase, surely one of the finest of its date in London, and admire its panache rather than worrying about whether a similar vocabulary, in other hands, would trash historic buildings elsewhere. We might even allow that the now

evident, and thoroughly predictable, leaks around the central copper rainwater pipes were a sign of the building ageing, acquiring valuable patina, rather than failure. We can applaud the increased attention to physical access for people with disabilities, the educational facilities, the commendable attempts to engage in work to bring in new audiences, all of which the lottery funding has helped to bring about.

We may still ponder how introspective a building can be. Will it always be acceptable that the building has no access from the south and east? On these sides, the extension is barely visible from the public domain, because it is behind a virtually imperforate three metre high brick wall. Just as the almshouses closed in 1909, and the site was sold off because of a perception of the adverse impact of nasty neighbours, so in 1998 this wall kept the remaining outside industry away from the haven of the Museum. Now, of course, construction work is well advanced and very shortly the back of the museum and the new extension will be seen from the London Overground. The extension of the East London Line from Dalston to West Croydon is costing £1billion and will open in 2010. The nasty industry will have gone, but perhaps it is now time for the Museum to address the outside world.

But perhaps what we are most going to worry about is what will happen to history. The upper display gallery already includes an interior from the 1990s. The extension, by its very form and content, seems to be telling a story that history is at an end. However, there is now talk of another, even bigger extension, again in expectation of more lottery funding. So history is not yet at an end, and neither are the issues of contextual design, which this time will include the need to design in harmony with both parts of the museum.

Far left: The well-detailed and magnificent staircase in the new extension.

Above: The back elevation of the 'inaccessible' 18th-century almshouses can be seen to the left of the extension, with the railway line to the right.

Anthony Thistleton

Haggerston School for Girls

Weymouth Terrace E2

Architect Ernö Goldfinger 1964-7 | listed Grade II

Walking along Queensbridge Road, just north of the canal, it is easy to pass without note a long 1960s building tucked behind trees and a mish-mash of small huts, ball courts and parked cars. The strong rectilinear form and the classical proportions struggle hard to catch the eye, and the impression might be of another run-down concrete block, in need of repair or perhaps replacement.

Upon closer inspection, however, the quality of materials and proportion, the form and meticulous attention to detail reveal a building of refinement and elegance. This is the work of a master Modernist, an architect of maturity and conviction. This is the work of Ernö Goldfinger.

For Goldfinger, one's perception of a building was integral to his approach and he identified three distinct ways in which observers understood and responded to architecture. These were from a

distance, as an object or sculpture; pictorially, as an elevation or façade; and finally as a space, as an all-encompassing and multi-sensory experience, including sound, smell and memory as well as sight and touch. It is through exploring these three aspects in relation to the school that we can best understand his approach and appreciate the building itself.

As an object, the main classroom block, at four-storeys, almost 300 feet by 50 feet, dominates the site. It acts as a spine from which two satellite buildings project, forming the entrance and ancillary spaces to the west and a gym to the east. From the air, the logic of the organisation becomes clear, but at ground level the juxtaposition of these solid annex blocks to the intricate filigree of the fenestration of the main block forms a dramatic contrast, and transforms the view of the school from each angle. Reinforcing this elemental arrangement, a water

Far left: The main classroom block, before refurburbishment with rooftop water tower and classrooms.

Above: Interior of main entrance hall with its warm timber panelling.

tower flanked by two rooftop classrooms, sits atop the main block, marking the entrance axis. A small square caretaker's house sits to the north of the site, completely separate from the main buildings, yet very much a part of the overall composition.

As one moves closer and explores the static façade, the two-dimensional surface design becomes apparent. A rigid order emerges across the teaching block, comprising 17 bays with floor slabs expressed as narrow bands in bush-hammered concrete while the columns are broad and smooth faced. The resultant order is broken on the west elevation by the library, which projects at first floor level along almost half the length of the building, with full height glazing and louvred screens. On the eastern façade, the main cross axes linking the satellite buildings are marked by a change in fenestration, and further projections to the north of the building house classrooms for each year.

This planar approach – effectively a design in two-and-a-half dimensions – is echoed in Goldfinger's better-known Trellick Tower in North Kensington, which followed the completion of Haggerston School. Here also the elevations reveal the design process – a composition of detail and ratio leading to a honed and balanced façade. The use of order and reliance on the golden section is doubtless a relic from the architect's Beaux-Arts training.

Moving inside the building, one can appreciate Goldfinger's concern with stimulating all the senses. While after years of adaptation and intensive use much of the building's original detailing has been lost, the strength and clarity of his original design prevails and the main spaces are still recognisable and retain their character.

The magnificent main entrance hall, for example, with its coffered concrete ceiling and warm timber panelling, or the library with its opening louvres, remain spaces that evoke a strong emotional response and still echo the original intent.

The intervening years have not been particularly kind to the school, with a number of amendments and additions. These range from the benign – enclosing the walkways and overcoating the exposed concrete – to the less excusable bland single-storey brick and pitched roofed annexes that have sprouted from the main block.

The original design was not perfect either, with the south-facing classrooms becoming unusable in summer. However, the school remains popular with teachers and students, and it is now subject to further refurbishment and adaptation through the erstwhile Building Schools for the Future programme. There is, perhaps, reason to be more optimistic as the architects selected to restore Haggerston School also refurbished Goldfinger's house at Willow Road in Hampstead. Avanti Architects' proposals involve a rethinking of the layout of the main block to incorporate new approaches to teaching and the addition of a new satellite, echoing an original proposal by Goldfinger, to house specialised teaching facilities. Through examining these proposals, it becomes evident that the original concept is strong enough to accommodate both the changing needs and these new works without diminishing the building's clear identity.

Haggerston School for Girls, Goldfinger's only secondary school project, was preceded by two much smaller primary schools, built in the early 1950s in Wandsworth and Hammersmith. Goldfinger's limited number of school projects belies his passionate belief in education, his own experience as a keen student from an early age and a vehement proselytiser throughout his life.

Towards the end of the war, Goldfinger co-authored a popular book interpreting the new *County of London Plan* commissioned by the London County Council. While the LCC Architects' Department, which reached its peak at 3,000 staff in 1956, was responsible for much of the post-war building work, the schools department was much smaller and tended to handle schools' maintenance while sub-contracting design work to private architects. The legacy of this approach is a series of unique, compelling and experimental buildings that embody optimism in the uplifting and civilising power of education. Sadly, many of these, such as John Bancroft's recently demolished Pimlico School, are now lost.

Ernö Goldfinger is one of a number of 20th-century architects whose work is denounced by many while celebrated by architects and other 'cognoscenti'. His uncompromising rational approach led to buildings that are emblematic of their era and now are, often wrongly, associated with the wider social problems that they harbour. It is gratifying to note that Haggerston School for Girls, along with Goldfinger's two primary schools, was listed Grade II in 2004, joining his Balfrom and Trellick Towers that had been given this honour and protection eight years previously.

Left: Main entrance of corridor with its coffered concrete ceiling. Avanti Architects intend to restore the character of Goldfinger's original design.

Tim Ronalds

Hothouse

Richmond Road E8

Architect Ash Sakula Architects 2003 and 2007

An almost hidden gem

In the north-east corner of London Fields near the railway viaduct there is a children's playground. Behind the swings behind the trees stands an intriguing and beautiful new building. A boomerang-shaped three-storey wall embraces the playground. Amoeba-shaped windows are scattered over its soft pink brick surface. It looks most fascinating at dusk when light emanates from the bubbly windows dancing above and below a horizontal band of glass which runs from end to end. Inside you can see an enormous single studio space.

It is only from London Fields that you can really see the building. To get in you have to go round to Richmond Road or Martello Street, where you find on either street metal mesh gates which lead into a yard beside the railway viaduct and signs which announce that this is the Hothouse.

Hothouse was built for and by Free Form Arts Trust and designed by Ash Sakula Architects. Free Form was a creative regeneration agency and their new building was to be a centre for community-based regeneration through the arts and cultural industries. It took its name from the 'Loddiges – the largest hothouses in the world' that once stood on the site. The centre contains a gallery and conference space, workspaces for artists, a huge shared studio for creative enterprises, and a rooftop terrace with more studios. The adjoining railway arches are workspaces for creative industries. The exploitation of a marginal site like this, to make something creative, optimistic and beautiful, is a wonderful example of the best things that have been happening in Hackney over the last decade.

Do dare to venture in. You will find Free Form welcoming and happy to show you around. The building is imbued with creative spirit and fun in

Far left: Exterior with amoeba-shaped windows.

Above: First-floor office space for Free Form Arts Trust.

every part. Each element has been reinvented simply and practically, but in an original and unusual way – a provocation to think of something new yourself. Triffid-like lights grow out of the ceiling over the reception desk; plywood panels slot into boxes to allow the space to be re-shaped.

 A wood-lined staircase winds up to the first floor where you emerge into the most spectacular space of the Hothouse: its main studio. This is a huge curving double-height room, with a continuous window at desktop height giving a panoramic view through the trees and across London Fields. Above, the bubbly windows drop patches of sunlight onto the floor, and on the back wall a mezzanine balcony clad in white corrugated plastic zig-zags the length of the studio. A double-height window, at either end of the space, draws your eye through, and every now and then a train on the viaduct appears to slice right through the room. The space has a scale and generosity that makes it a perfect setting for the creative and collaborative work of the enterprises that share it.

Going up again, the staircase leads to a rooftop gallery: a light, silver structure made of steel and

Above: Exterior as viewed from London Fields. The railway line runs behind the building.

glass with photovoltaic cells which generate electricity and dappled light. One side of the gallery leads to more studio workspaces, the other opens onto a huge wooden roof terrace which extends over the whole of the roof of the main studio.

Here, up between the treetops and the overhead wires of the railway tracks is a wonderful outdoor space for exhibitions, events, activities and growing things. The trains rush past, close and fast, squealing like a bacon slicer as they take the curve.

This was not an expensive building, quite the reverse, and was built with complex grant funding raised over a long period by the efforts of dedicated and altruistic people. The building feels generous and full of light and space. Every part, every detail is stimulating, and Ash Sakula's design embodies a sense of humanity and creativity that is an inspiration.

2013 update:
Since this was written, Free Form Arts has gone into liquidation.

Tim Horsey

In-Between

Whatcott's Yard N16

Architect Riches Ullmayer and Garibaldo 2003

In-Between is a radical modern take on the traditional housing terrace so common throughout the borough of Hackney. It is a row of three individual houses built over the period 2001-3 between the existing Victorian terraces of Palatine Road and Brighton Road in Stoke Newington. The building is situated in Whatcott's Yard, a former storage yard, and is reached through a narrow alley opposite the junction of Allen Road and Nevill Road – it is almost invisible from the street.

The building is functional and Modernist in style, with strong and simple lines, and its front façade, which slopes 7 per cent from the vertical, is made entirely of glass. The flat roof, which is perpendicular to the front face, has a slight pitch towards the rear of the building. It is entirely timber-framed, which allows for great flexibility in the interior design and made for relative ease of construction.

In-Between was designed by the international partnership of Annalie Riches (English), Silvia Ullmayer (German) and Barti Garibaldo (Italian), who met on the Diploma in Architecture course at the University of North London. Each had been practising for some years with other architects before this collaboration. The building, their first and only joint project, was designed primarily as a place for each of them to live, and built at relatively modest cost of £125,000 for each house, with an additional £120,000 paid for the site.

Ullmayer, who still lives in the middle house, describes their achievement as "making a dream come true in a rapidly rising property market." To do this, she explains, "it was necessary to design a building by committee which was able to meet the individual needs and desires of each member of the group at relatively low cost." At the outset the three collaborators agreed to maintain their commitment to ownership of the project for a

Above: The almost-invisible west elevation of the three houses.

minimum of five years from the start, but all are still living at In-Between – a testament to the success of the project.

The building was completed in 2003 and went on to receive a Future House London Award, an RIBA Award and, more recently, the prestigious *Architects' Journal* First Building Award. Since its completion Silvia Ullmayer's partnership with Allan Sylvester has been responsible for two other innovative projects in Hackney: Minihome nursery on Allen Road, Stoke Newington; and the New Summerhouse, also in Stoke Newington. The architects were very keen to mirror the surrounding terraced-housing typology with In-Between, as they believe this gives strength and unity to the design, making it much more than the sum of its individual parts.

Although each of the three houses has the same internal area of 47m², and are externally identical, their interior spaces are arranged completely differently. No.1 is a combined house and workspace, no. 2 a two-bedroom house and no. 3 has two self-contained flats. Behind the identical façades, the timber-framed construction has allowed for contrasting layouts of light and open spaces. Individual touches include a trapeze for Riches and a double-height bathroom with a skylight above the bath for Ullmayer.

The internal variations were made possible by constructing a frame for the two main storeys, between which mezzanine levels and different room layouts were fitted. In some places the ceiling heights stretch to six metres, a remarkable luxury for such small-scale dwellings, and the houses also succeed in achieving a feeling of space as a result of the outward-looking

perspectives of many of the rooms – in dramatic contrast to the outlooks of their Victorian forebears. Many of the room layouts and sizes are unorthodox, but the construction methods allow them to be altered very easily in future, as the internal partitions are formed of light-weight polycarbonate.

The architects made a point of using sustainable materials for this new building. The terrace is constructed from Parallam-laminated timber posts and beams. These are strengthened wooden beams which can bear heavy loads but which are also visually appealing when exposed. The beams are relatively light in weight, which made handling easier during the building process – an important issue for the architects, who undertook much of the construction work themselves to keep costs to a minimum.

The homes use recycled newspaper and sheep's wool for insulation, and there is a green roof planted with sedum, which should protect the felt roof from sun damage and in time develop its own eco-system. It was intended that the houses should be as energy efficient as possible, and this partly determined their south-facing aspect. Thermostat-controlled under-floor heating runs throughout.

Whatcott's Yard was the only site Riches, Ullmayer and Garibaldo could find in north-east London which was large enough to allow the integration of this kind of innovation into a traditional residential urban setting. Hackney Council's decision to change its planning-use status from light industrial to residential resulted in the borough gaining this pioneering and award-winning example of domestic architecture.

Far left: Living room with sliding doors leading to bedroom. A mezzanine level is accommodated thanks to the high ceiling heights.

Above left: Kitchen.

Above: Exterior showing elevation which slopes 7 per cent from the vertical.

Geraldine Bedell

Mossbourne Community Academy

Downs Park Road E5

Architect Rogers Stirk Harbour and Partners 2004; extension by Studio E Architect 2009

Mossbourne Community Academy occupies a site that was once notorious. In the 1990s, Hackney Downs School, a comprehensive described by the government and in the press as 'the worst school in Britain' was one of the first in the country to be shut down under the school closures programme.

As a boys' grammar school, the former Hackney Downs School had produced playwrights and politicians – Harold Pinter and Steven Berkoff, Lord Levy and Lord Peston. The comprehensive that replaced it in 1974 took up some of Hackney's biggest social challenges: more than 70 per cent of children spoke English as a second language and over 50 per cent came from households with no one in employment.

The school developed a reputation for unruliness and chaos, rolls fell dramatically, and the school was finally closed in 1995.

In 2004, a brand new building designed by Rogers Stirk Harbour and Partners opened its doors to 200 eleven-year-olds. There was a lot riding on Mossbourne: it was one of the earliest of the government's City Academies, which were in the vanguard of a highly political attempt to galvanise state education by removing schools from local authority control. Academies were to be backed by a sponsor – in this case the transport millionaire, East Ender Sir Clive Bourne, who named the school after his father – and to be given much greater freedom over the curriculum.

Mossbourne was opened by the then-Prime Minister, Tony Blair, and is the school that's credited with having persuaded his successor, Gordon Brown, to stick with the Academies programme. The leader of the opposition, David Cameron, launched the Conservatives' education policy here. It is everyone's favourite school, or at least, every politician's.

Far left: Exterior detailing galvanised steel staircase and timber-framed structure on west wing.

Above: Assembly hall and auditorium located at the apex of the 'V'. Splashes of red are used on the wall and the acoustic panelling on the ceiling.

The success of Mossbourne has been staggering. The latest Ofsted inspection judged the school outstanding in every respect; the inspectors said they were enthralled by the hard work and dedication of the teaching staff and the attitude to learning of the pupils. The Key Stage 3 value-added results are the best in the country: Mossbourne students made more than four terms' progress above the national norm. This has been achieved despite the decision not to exercise the school's right, as an Academy, to select 10 per cent of its pupils on ability.

The social problems faced by the pupils have not evaporated simply because they attend school in a spanking new building: 40 per cent are on free school meals; and 35 per cent are on the special educational needs register, with 55 of those having SEN statements, meaning that they have the most severe problems, 19 of whom have autism. The surrounding area is still troubled by gangs and drugs, and teachers feel it is necessary to escort children onto buses at the end of the day, and to patrol the streets in pairs.

Successful schools are led by headteachers with vision, who are capable of attracting first-class, energetic teachers, and the success of Mossbourne is due in very large part to the Principal, Sir Michael Wilshaw, and his team. But the buildings (in whose design Sir Michael was involved) have also played their part. There are schools around the country that have been designed by big-name architects but that don't seem to articulate any educational philosophy, beyond perhaps a desire to make schools look more like businesses. But at Mossbourne, Rogers Stirk Harbour and Partners have created a building that reflects the partnership's position as one of the outstanding international practices, responsible for decades of exciting work, from the Centre Pompidou to Madrid Barajas Airport, Lloyd's of London to the National Assembly for Wales.

The site was awkward, quite apart from its associations: a triangle bounded on two sides by railway lines, and to the north by a road and the parkland of Hackney Downs. The architects dealt with it by making the building V-shaped, wedged into the apex of the triangle against a bright blue wall of masonry that shields the school from the railway lines and creates a barrier against the noise of the trains.

This orientates the school around the playground and towards the park, with the classrooms all facing outwards, north east and north west, so maximising daylight while minimising glare. Not unusually for a building from this team of architects, the structure is exposed: Mossbourne

Above: Triple-height atrium classroom with shade umbrellas.

is one of the largest timber-framed buildings in the UK, with tall, chunky columns extending three-storeys, from ground to roof, supporting rafters and floor beams. The wood is warm and creates an impression of solidity and of something enduring and sustainable.

Galvanised steel balconies lace the first and second floors, facing the playground, and four staircases are suspended from these to the ground. At this level there is a covered cloister area, creating sheltered outdoor space and a route between the vertical terraced 'houses' that are given over to different subjects – boldly indicated with vinyl lettering on the windows.

Inside, the rear of the building features a top-lit atrium, with space for IT and for breakout areas from the classrooms, sheltered by large café umbrellas. Considerable thought was given to trying to reduce the number of potential spaces where bullying could occur: communal areas are open and designed to be easily supervised; toilets have only three cubicles; and children move around under the watchful eye of staff, who demand high standards of discipline, allowing pupils to feel safe.

In the apex of the 'V' sit drama and music departments on the ground floor, plus a double-height hall on the first floor with an acoustic ceiling. There are splashes of colour throughout: a red wall in the main hall; a yellow one in the sports hall; and colour on the doors of the 'houses'. This is a building that is not afraid to make a bold statement. Yet because of its orientation on the site, its discretion, and its attention to durability and sustainability, it still fits un-fussily into its surroundings. The detailing is finely crafted; this is a lovely space to move around in, to stand in the playground and look at. The pupils can feel proud that so much care has been taken over their place.

The interior is light and full of interesting spaces. For security reasons, the school is not as open to the community as the architects would have liked, or as one can hope it might yet become. A high and forbidding iron fence separates it from the street and the park. But for the children who attend Mossbourne, the building embodies a sense of inclusion, security and belonging. It doesn't feel conventional, cheap, thrown-up or second-rate. The pupils can see every morning as they arrive at school that they matter enough to have this building, and that knowledge must have contributed significantly to the national success-story that the school has become.

Amin Taha

Rivington Place

Rivington Place EC2A

Architect Adjaye Associates 2007

Rivington Place is a new visual arts centre in Shoreditch, and the first new-build public gallery in London since the completion of the Hayward Gallery in 1968. It opened on 3 October 2007 and is home to two charities promoting artists of diverse ethnicities: the Institute of International Visual Arts (Iniva) and Autograph (ABP). This beautiful new building designed by Adjaye Associates houses a public gallery, lecture theatre, café, the Stuart Hall Library and administrative offices. It is a hive of activity on a compact site in the heart of London's contemporary art scene.

David Adjaye OBE, the principal architect, is one of Britain's most admired architects, having been short-listed for the Stirling Prize in 2006 and with a number of other major commissions to his name. To some his rise is attributed to his colour, perhaps in part and why not? As a black architect he remains fairly singular in the profession, as one who is as confident and relaxed in his ability to produce striking designs as he is of deserving interest.

Adjaye's commissions include major buildings, interiors for a national high street bank, as well as graphics, clothing and furniture. His practice has developed its own coherent and identifiable brand, likened to Foster and Partners for their generation, and there lies the context for this building, this kind of architecture and the debate it generates. For Adjaye has already been pooled with Rem Koolhas, Zaha Hadid and Frank Gehry as part of the 'bad gang'. At Rivington Place the inventiveness, applied at every turn in one of their earlier houses, is scaled up by investigating the reading of the building in the townscape and the journey from street to internal public spaces.

The building's immediacy works. One's first impression is of a monolithic mass accentuated by

Above: Ground floor gallery space.

its slot windows with a dark saw-tooth-sculpted skyline. Robust and self assured, it gives the clients' new institutional home a sense of permanence. The façade is skilfully achieved by breaking it into what appear to be blocks allowed to slip past one another towards a chequer-board pattern, but with enough overlap to emphasise a sense of their interlocking through friction.

The opened gaps reveal a depth of half a meter or so to glazed windows, with some of the glazing brought forward to be flush. The pattern varies in vertical coursing, dense and narrow on the main street and broadening at the building's corner and to the rear, generating a robust – almost defensive – depth. That may have led to the interesting decision to subvert the visual sense of gravity by replacing a considerable length of the ground floor with full-height clear glazing without mullions, making the ground floor gallery an inviting shop window onto Rivington Street. The concept is further broken down at the rear, where the blocks hang in mid-air and are carved out for delivery access, their pattern then slightly continued onto the rendered back wall.

The main entrance is through the lower side door in Rivington Place which opens into the double-height lobby and desk control point, though on certain occasions direct entry into the gallery is available from Rivington Street. The block system is represented internally through glazed openings, timber-lined ingle-nooks that aid the sense of intimacy in the library and office layouts and in some areas where back lighting substitutes windows. Altogether, is it then a reoccupied and

reused castle body revealing a grander volume and intent? The floors and ceiling successfully aim for the stripped-down appearance employed at the 'Idea Stores' where the robustness of the public street identifies the informality within.

In some areas it is let down by poor craftsmanship. The entrance lobby could have benefited from less, and certainly better, plasterboard construction which – part enclosing the wall, part the stair and balustrade – shrinks the space and dilutes the necessary transition from the external theme. Different-coloured paint junctions, having no shadow gap or material threshold, rely on meandering brush strokes. The plastering of the handrail adjacent to the front desk is finished by a confused hand with unconvincing geometry. Some ambitious flush door-to-wall detailing hasn't been installed satisfactorily, contrasting with those areas that remain simple with fewer material junctions which suit and elevate their spaces.

Perhaps like a young Foster or Stirling, Adjaye will continue to innovate and develop a detail catalogue suitable to budget and contract type. On the whole Rivington Place achieves a successful branding identity for its clients, and provides a range of workshop spaces, education facilities, offices, library, café and meeting places, not to mention two important gallery areas which have established a strong foothold for a wide range of culturally-diverse artists already enjoying an international reputation. As such it is a convincing and welcome addition to the townscape, to Hackney's and the UK's built and social heritage.

Far left: Inviting shopfront window of gallery facing onto Rivington Place.

Above left: Top-floor office space.

Above: Defence-like exterior.

Cathy Strongman

Rowe Lane

Rowe Lane E9

Architect FLACQ Architects 2005-6

Tucked down an inconspicuous cobbled lane in the throbbing heart of Hackney is a house designed by Marcus Lee, director of FLACQ Architects, which challenges prevailing attitudes about the methods, materials and technologies used to design residential buildings within urban settings. Constructed almost entirely from prefabricated timber parts, the 250m^2 house, which cost £300,000 and took 16 weeks to build, is dripping with sustainable features. As such it provides valuable lessons about how we can meet Britain's spiralling housing needs and environmental targets. Equally it offers a practical, spacious and light-filled home that Lee designed for himself and his family.

The interior and exterior of the house imbue a sense of elegant simplicity, yet this clarity has been achieved through complex engineering. The fundamental aim behind the project was to create a timber system that would ensure fast, efficient and straightforward construction, and provide flexibility once the building was complete. Working closely with timber-frame specialist Gordon Cowley and the engineer and design consulting firm Arup, Lee created a bespoke timber-frame kit that is assembled using Cowley Connectors – specially-developed stainless steel connections that are entirely hidden from view. Lee, who cites the Eames House, Walter Seagal and Japanese architecture among his influences, admits to being obsessed by timber-frames. Unlike most modern houses, where the frame is disguised behind plasterboard, here the Siberian larch structure is exposed both outside and in.

Lee decided on a Siberian larch because it is a highly durable wood grown in sustainably-managed forests. This is just one of the building's many eco credentials. The walls and roof have been lined with a 150mm-thick layer of flax insulation, which is a natural, renewable and

Far left: Kitchen.

Above: North elevation at night.

non-toxic product. Pavatherm insulating fibre-boards have been laid over this to provide even more insulation. These boards are a German product that have impressive insulating properties and do not contain any toxic glues or wood preservatives. On the exterior the entire building, including the roof, is clad in sustainably-grown cedar, with the door and window frames made from the same material. The entrance gate and the balconies are crafted from Douglas fir.

The house has been cleverly arranged so that all the storage and service areas are located around the perimeter, forming a buffer to the party walls and maximising space within. The structure has no internal load-bearing walls, which allowed Lee to carve up the interior spaces with demountable partitioning walls that can be reconfigured as the demands of his family evolve. The ground floor is almost entirely open plan, with vast glazed areas visually connecting the interiors to the front courtyard and the garden behind. Glass doors at either end of the property can be opened in the summer to cross-ventilate the space. The lower section of the slanted roof, which leans over the kitchen, is entirely glazed and draws natural light into the ground floor areas. In the summer this is partially shaded by the trees on the site, but in the winter, when these trees lose their leaves, the sun helps passively to heat the home. The first and second floors have smaller windows and are divided to provide bedrooms.

Above: Living, dining and kitchen areas.

Above right: Staircase.

Walls and ceilings throughout the house have been finished with lime plaster and porous paints. These are non-toxic materials that permit the timber walls to breath, therefore preventing damp and rot. The floors in the living areas are laid with slate, which is easy to clean, hardwearing and has a high thermal mass, which allows it to store the sun's energy during the day and release it into the building as the temperature cools at night. Upstairs, carpets have been installed and all the floors have been equipped with underfloor heating which is connected to a wood pellet boiler. Lee is currently exploring the idea of adding solar panels to the south-west roof to heat the water.

Through his choice of materials and meticulous planning and detailing, Lee has managed to create an exciting, aesthetically pleasing, environmentally conscious and comfortable family home, which was affordable to build and is inexpensive to run. As the needs of his family change, the building can be adapted at minimal cost and without disruptive building work. If the house is ever abandoned, it can be dismantled and either rebuilt or recycled.

It is rare to see timber buildings among the brick-dominated streets of Hackney, and yet the house on Rowe Lane slips effortlessly into its surroundings. As the cedar-cladding starts to age and turn a silvery grey, it will become even more at one with its garden setting. It is a project that clearly demonstrates the benefits of timber as a fast, effective, economical and also sustainable construction material. It is also yet another example of the innovative spirit that continues to infect the buildings of Hackney and which makes its mélange of buildings so eclectic and exciting.

Kevin Moore

Truman's Road

Truman's Road N16

Architect Dominic Cullinan and Ivan Harbour 1996

This pair of semi-detached houses were designed and built by Dominic Cullinan and Ivan Harbour as homes for themselves and their families.

Cullinan and Harbour were introduced by mutual friends who knew they were both looking to build their own houses. The original plan was to build two detached houses at either end of the plot, but after long discussions and several alternatives they settled on the form of the semi-detached house. Planning permission was granted in 1989, but the build was not completed until 1996. This was due to building work only taking place at weekends and during holidays – using family, friends and anyone else who was willing to be roped in to help. During this period both families were living on site. Cullinan and Harbour built as temporary residences one shed at the bottom of the garden and another under one of the main houses. The design for the surviving shed feels like

an early prototype for Mossbourne Community Academy – a subsequent building designed by Harbour in 2004 (see page 39).

The design of the two houses took a year. At the time the young architects were just starting out in their careers, with Cullinan working for Ian Ritchie Architects and Harbour working for Richard Rogers Partnership. They were mainly designing offices, and chose to reuse and recycle materials from their other building projects. The glazing bars and walls were left over from the European Court of Human Rights in Strasbourg – bringing a whole new meaning to liberation.

Cullinan and Harbour concealed the steel frame inside the outer walls and floors, and this frame also doubled up as a kind of scaffolding to facilitate the build. The material palette is strikingly simple: concrete, anodised aluminium, wood and glass; unlike the construction which was labour

Above: Exterior.

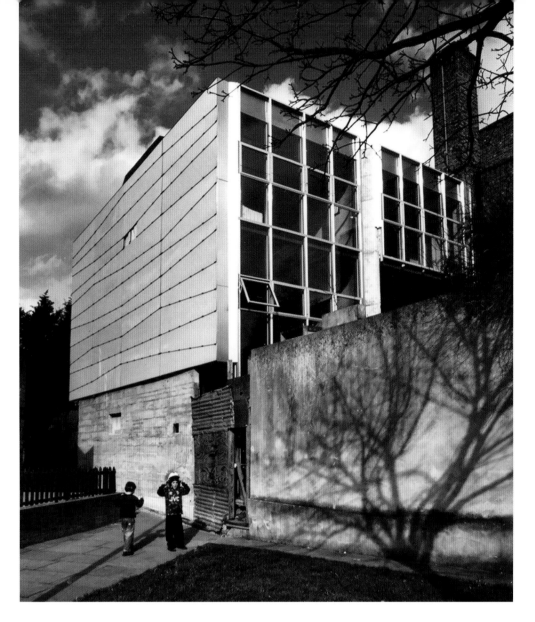

intensive and time consuming. The pouring and setting of the separate levels and parts of the concrete walls took months to prepare, and over two weeks for each pour to cure and set. The concrete, left exposed in most places, is a constant reminder of the heroic efforts taken to construct the building.

Each house has three storeys, with a timber and glass bedroom 'pod' on the roof taking full advantage of the views – especially the City to the south. There is also a small overhang on the frontage, which creates a further room on each of the first and second floors.

The staircase is ingenious, although not an original idea. The curving stairs are an elongated interlocking double helix based on the Château de Chambord in the Loire Valley, which is believed to have been designed by Leonardo da Vinci. This form also appears as unrealised drawings by Palladio and even earlier in a mosque by the Ottoman architect Sinan. Each staircase encroaches onto the neighbouring house, but is self-contained. Each reinforced concrete step, cast

in situ and resting on the step below, forms the heart of the two houses.

Cullinan told me that although he enjoyed the process he doesn't think he would have the energy to do it again. He also thought that the planners were very trusting at the time. "It was a very scary street so perhaps that limited the site visits!" At first the planners wanted a more traditional build as well "as drawings done with a ruler." Eventually the existing modern design was agreed upon.

Cullinan and Harbour progressively learnt how to work together, as they had never designed a building with each other before. The great benefit of working this way was that the burden and stresses were shared. Cullinan also said that he "felt utterly dependent on Harbour and no doubt he felt the same," and there was a huge sense of relief on completion of this very communal project. You could say their relationship was cast in the concrete of the house as they poured and waited for their shared staircase to dry.

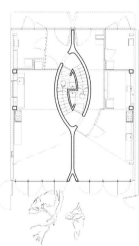

Far left: Concrete staircase.

Above left: Back elevation.

Above: Floor plan showing interlocking double helix.

Restored

historic buildings that have been saved

"[Hackney] is also an interesting place to explore a whole gamut of approaches to conservation and reuse of other types of buildings... Improvement is an uphill struggle."

Bridget Cherry and Nikolaus Pevsner, 'The Buildings of England', 1998

Left: Loggia-inspired theatre boxes, Hackney Empire.

Chris Miele

91-101 Worship Street

Worship Street EC2

Architect Philip Webb 1861 | restoration unknown *c.*1990 | listed Grade II*

In 1861 Philip Webb (1831-1915) designed these six 'live-work' units for a philanthropist, Major William Gillum. Each had a rear workshop (now demolished), a small shop at the front and a maisonette above.

Gillum built them to rent to local artisans and their families who were poorly housed. Like so many model developments, this socially progressive agenda had no real influence. In the end only prosperous tradesmen could afford the rent. Still, the history and architecture of the Worship Street buildings speak volumes about the local area and progressive Victorian design.

In 1858 Webb designed Red House in Bexley-heath for William Morris. Webb would go on to work with Morris at Morris, Marshall, Faulkner & Co (founded in 1861). The Worship Street buildings also reflect the awakening social conscience that would lead Webb eventually to Socialism.

Shoreditch was then renowned for the mass production of furniture. But this industrial process was not concentrated in the hands of a few large-scale manufacturers, each operating from a substanial complex of buildings housing different processes. Instead industrial production relied on smaller, independent and complementary businesses. In early 19th-century Shoreditch, individual joiners, carvers, polishers and upholsterers contributed to the manufacture of a range of furniture to a specification provided by wholesalers.

Initially, the trade made use of modest terraced 18th-century housing common across Hoxton, Shoreditch, Haggerston and Bethnal Green. Following an older pattern people lived and worked in the same building. By the 1860s and 1870s speculators began to develop purpose-built workshops or manufactories. Many were small and mean, fitted into older, narrow terraced plots. This type of building had wrought iron or steel lintels

Far left: Front elevation showing boarded-up shopfronts, 1945.

Above: Interior workshop looking towards the back, 1971.

spanning large windows. A good example of this can be seen at nos. 16-26 Rivington Street. Larger, speculative workshops of more traditional industrial character also date from this period – nos. 65-83 Leonard Street and nos. 43-9 Charlotte Street are particularly fine examples of this type.

Gillum's development replaced older properties, which, according to the 1851 Census, were inhabited by more than 100 people. In August 1863 *The Builder* described these houses as "miserable, ill-ventilated, tumble-down buildings" and "wretched tenements". The magazine also recorded that an ancestor of Gillum had purchased the property in 1765. Furthermore, 'Gillum's Fields' (as the tenements were known) was the spot where "Shakespeare was accustomed to take charge of citizens who had gone in to see the performances at the Curtain Road theatre." Afterwards, during the English Civil War, it had been a depot for Parliamentary forces.

Gillum's patronage of the arts was quite significant. In 1860 he commissioned Webb to design a gardener's cottage at his large property, the Moated House, in Tottenham; and according to Nikolaus Pevsner Gillum commissioned Webb to design some furniture. He also patronised the Pre-Raphaelite painters Ford Maddox Brown and Dante Gabriel Rossetti. Brown's beautiful view of Walton-on-the-Naze was in Gillum's collection.

The design of 91-101 Worship Street is very subtle. What catches the eye are the small-paned, timber shopfronts (a rejection of the new style of plate glass shopfronts then being installed in the larger showrooms nearby). Instead of mass-produced slate roofs – the London norm – there are clay plain tiles more at home in Sussex than the East End. On the first floor, a pair of sitting-room windows are brought together under a single

Above: Front elevation with restored small-paned timber shopfronts, 2009.

Gothic arch. Webb had trained in the office of the great Victorian Gothic architect George Edmund Street. The arch is a reminder of this background.

On the second floor Webb varied the rhythm of openings: three smaller windows sit neatly on a stone string course, which is continuous across the terrace. This feature locks the buildings together visually. Above is a steeply pitched roof with prominent stacks of early 18th-century proportions, not a shallow roof formed of short timber spans hiding behind a parapet, again as would be the norm in London. Within the roof is an over-scaled, hipped dormer. All these completely alien features recede into a background of standard London stock-facing brick, laid not in standard Flemish bond, but in the more vernacular English bond commonly found on buildings of the Weald in Kent.

The terrace also has one very unusual feature, which records its progressive intent. At the eastern boundary, and bedded into an odd, buttress-like structure built out from the wall of no. 101, is a public drinking fountain set in granite. Workmen almost exclusively relied on beer and gin, with sad results. Fresh water was a mark of enlightened urban planning, improvements to public health and the budding Temperance movement.

Here are not just the seeds of Webb's mature style. In one small project he demonstrates wit, a feeling for proportion, and a willingness to subvert accepted forms. All these tricks find their way back to his Gothic Revival training, but taken together these features become more elemental. His design stands somewhere between traditional, representational architecture and the sort of abstraction for which Mackintosh and Voysey are perhaps better known.

Allen Abramson

The Castle Climbing Centre

Green Lanes N4

Architects William Chadwell Mylne with Robert Billings 1856 | refurbishment designs by Nicholas Grimshaw and Partners 1995 and Cook Townsend Architects 2005 | listed Grade II

A Castle in the Suburbs

Enter Clissold Park from Stoke Newington Church Street, traverse this amiable green space in the direction of Brownswood Road, and gaze towards the skyline at the looming turrets and towers of the Castle Climbing Centre. Situated towards the southern end of Green Lanes, the Castle guards no lordly estate but a reservoir – or, to be more precise, two reservoirs – with one immediately behind its eastern ramparts and one half a mile away on the other side of Lordship Road. On its western side, the imposing brickwork of the Castle nowadays dominates traffic passing between Stamford Hill and Blackstock Road. Across the road is a small area of recently erected flats, on the site of former filter beds.

Of course, this most feudal of Stoke Newington's buildings is nothing of the sort. It was commissioned by the New River Company, in 1856, as the second of two pumping stations built inside a 90-acre hydraulic complex fed by the New River – which can still be seen skirting the grounds. Begun in 1831 on the site of a brickworks, the complex included: the East and West Reservoirs; a gas-house equipped to introduce chlorine to the water; filter beds; two pumping stations (the one on Lordship Road was demolished in 1905); and in 1936 a filtration plant, built in an imposing Modernist style. (See Monica Blake's article, page 78.)

The first pumping station, constructed in 1833, was squat and rectangular, sporting a tall cylindrical tower covering its functional chimney. Classical exteriors concealed its mechanical insides in a familiar and unobtrusive manner. It was, therefore, in complete architectural contrast, that the second of the two pumping stations punctured the Stoke Newington skyline as an outlandish folly modelled on a grand fortification.

Above: Interior view showing man climbing on wall with artificial features and hand holds, 2009.

In fact, the Castle Pumping Station was built in the wake of a severe cholera epidemic in 1850, and in response to the strict demands of the Metropolitan Water Act of 1852. Connected to a newer system of filter beds, the Castle had to deliver a more elaborate and more powerful mechanism than its predecessor. It housed the pipes, beams and fly-wheels of three steam engines (replaced only in 1942 by electric generators) rather than the single engine installed in the first station, leading to a single chimney poised conspicuously some 50 feet above the roof. Coal-sheds, a boiler-house and a workshop completed the Castle on its northern side.

No doubt, this giant pumping station could have been housed in as classical a carapace as its smaller predecessor. However, local protest ensured that the stark intrusiveness of its machinery be hidden and disguised. What emerged was an architectural solution that satisfied local taste yet still supported the technology. The chimney became the loftiest of three soaring towers; the great fly-wheels were simultaneously held and ensconced by jutting buttresses outside; and the whole edifice was raised on an earthen mound – as castles must be raised – ennobling the structure but also ensuring that condensation would return to sunken boilers rather than being transferred to the engine room. The pumping station was born as an industrial castle in seeming defiance of its intense, inner modernity. However, a quick trip around the British Isles – not to mention the British Empire – would have revealed that turrets and towers in

public works had roots not only in residential sensitivities, but also in governmental sensibilities. Victorian suspension bridges, reservoir dams and even hydro hotels were all metaphorically over-determined by signs of medieval might and grandeur, just as Victorian town halls, not to mention Westminster itself, were designed as veritable palaces of administration. These public exteriors effortlessly feudalised the phantasy of science, technology and governance, setting it impregnable in the 'modern' Victorian mind.

Commissioned by the New River Company, this industrial Castle was designed by an architect of Scottish origin, William Chadwell Mylne, in conjunction with Robert Billings. Mylne looked northwards for prototypes: more precisely to Billings, author of *The Baronial and Ecclesiastical Buildings of Scotland* (published in 1845-52). His other work included the restoration of Stirling Castle and Edinburgh Castle; and he was generally acknowledged as being at the forefront of the Scottish Baronial style (linked to the Gothic Revival). The 'castle' of Mylne and Billings drew eclectically from these real forebears. The chimney tower is polygonal; the standpipe is encased in a steepled tower topped with a broader square upper-storey; while the north-eastern corner of the roof morphs into a trim circular tower, capped by an elegant cone. Thin tall windows imply slots for archers, while the three flying buttresses are more ecclesiastical in design.

In those days, Revival appeared as 'folly'. In latter-day Hackney, by contrast, this big manifestation of

Far left: Spiral staircase located in the former chimney. Nowadays, it is used to practise abseiling, 2009.

Left: View of the engine house of the former Green Lanes Pumping Station from the south-east, 1860.

Above: Interior view showing original beams, fly-wheels and bouldering walls, 2009.

mock-medieval civility comes across not as simulacrum, but as a lynchpin of the borough's architectural heterogeneity and historical variegation. The same is true of its contemporary interior. Just as Victorian architects appropriated medieval motifs to make the Castle work to order and fit to signify in its own social time, so today have various actors successfully conspired to re-appropriate the Castle long after the pumping station has been retired and, for the most part, its machinery eviscerated. Thus, today, its huge inner space is far from being redundant. Since 1995, seeing off monstrous threats of its re-birth as a retail park, the Castle has sported an indoor climbing wall (indeed, one to rival the best in Europe). Making fine geometrical use of the Castle's spacious keep, synthetic slabs, walls, caves and buttresses test the strength and balance of climbing bodies, while the length of the great chimney tower confines a sheer vertical drop, perfect for abseil training and related rope-work. Just as the Tate Gallery, for example, rescued and embellished one great industrial space for artistic installation and exhibition, so the Castle Climbing Centre has done similarly for the exertions and art of climbing. With this surprising – but perfectly attuned – shift in function, the Castle survives the transition into late-modernity, pumping water no more, but pumping muscle aplenty.

Clapton Portico Learning Centre

Linscott Road E5

Architect William Southcote Inman 1823-5 | restored by Brady Mallalieu Architects 2005 | listed Grade II

Nestled just off Lower Clapton Road is one of the most surprisingly incongruent buildings in Hackney. Appearing like the relic of a Greek temple, its monumental scale dominates the residential street leading to its gates. Known fondly as the Clapton Portico, this extraordinary fragment is all that remains of the building originally designed to house the London Orphan Asylum.

The London Orphan Asylum was a charity founded in 1813 by the nonconformist minister Dr Andrew Reed. Its mission was to care for destitute children who had lost either their father or indeed both parents, educating them for gainful employment. The Charity was aimed at respectable families; the father's previous income had to be confirmed, as did his death, the parents' marriage and the child's good health. Families who had sought relief from the workhouse were ineligible, as were those where the widow remarried. Children could only enter between the ages of 10 and 11, and were discharged after they turned 15. As a 'voting charity', supporters of the asylum would receive a number of votes relative to their financial contribution. These votes were cast to decide which children would be able to enter the asylum. A large one-off payment meant a child could enter without election – Queen Victoria paid 600 guineas so that the Prince of Wales could present a child in this way.

Initially the orphanage was run from rented accommodation, but Reed used his persuasive personality to raise funds for a new, purpose-built home. In 1820, the charity purchased eight acres in Clapton (on the site of the closed Hackney School) and launched an architectural competition for a new building. This was won by William Southcote Inman, a young and inexperienced architect whose entry was his first major scheme.

Above: London Orphan Asylum, pre-1870. The grand central portico is all that remains of the building.

Inman designed an elaborate building consisting of a lofty Greek Doric-columned portico that formed the focal point of the imposing neo-classical façade of a much larger complex of buildings. The unfluted columns are of stucco while the walls to the rear of the colonnade are brick with stucco pilasters. The grand portico was the orphanage's public face, as well as the entrance to the orphanage chapel, a freestanding Tuscan building that was linked, via open colonnades, to a U-shaped block of dormitories and classrooms to the rear. These functional two-storey blocks had simple brick pediments to their gable-ends and were built in brick with stucco dressings. They ranged around a central courtyard, which lay behind the chapel.

Despite costs escalating from a predicted £15,000 to an enormous £25,000, the building was described as "very ambitious although rather cheaply executed". After designing the London Orphan Asylum, Inman entered more architectural competitions, but without notable success. The Clapton Portico is the remains of his only known surviving building.

The Asylum continued to grow in popularity but this led to overcrowding, which had devastating consequences during the 1866 typhoid epidemic. Fifteen children died, with 200 children contracting the disease. Due to these deaths, continued overcrowding and the rapid development of Clapton, the charity decided to build a larger facility in the rural location of Watford in Hertfordshire.

After the charity's move in 1871, the building was used briefly by the Metropolitan Asylums Board, and the London and Suburban Land Company acquired part of the grounds. From 1871-81 the building lay empty, and in the early 1880s the forecourt to the building was sold and the Victorian houses on Linscott Road were built.

In 1882, General William Booth, founder of the Salvation Army, prayed to God that the way might be opened for acquiring the building. As a growing organisation, the Salvationists were in need of a larger headquarters. Purchased for £150,000, little more than the land value, the building was considered by Booth as "the biggest bargain in London". The rear of the chapel was demolished and the open courtyard filled by a 3,000-seat Congress Hall and National Training Barracks. This site became the spiritual home of the Salvation Army and its followers. From here, thousands of officers were commissioned and sent all over the world to work with the most impoverished. Many key events in the Army's history happened at the Congress Hall – in 1912

General William Booth's body lay in state for three days, receiving an estimated 150,000 mourners.

In 1928 the Salvation Army moved its training college to Denmark Hill in south-east London, but they continued to use the hall for large events. In 1969 the buildings were purchased by the London Borough of Hackney to extend Clapton Girls' School. Despite being listed Grade II by English Heritage in 1975, the rest of the building was demolished, leaving just the portico, chapel and connecting colonnades.

The Clapton Portico, as the remaining ruin became known, was little more than a folly in the grounds of the school. Rapidly deteriorating, it became a long-standing feature on English Heritage's 'Buildings at Risk' register.

Fortunately, that was not the end of the building's remarkable history. In 1999 the artist Martin Creed installed *Work no. 203* across the frieze of the building. The artwork proclaimed in large neon text: EVERYTHING IS GOING TO BE ALRIGHT. Creed later confessed the overwhelmingly positive message was made during a period of personal depression, and was meant literally.

Creed's optimism appears to have been well founded, at least for the Clapton Portico. Thanks to grants from the Heritage Lottery Fund and the Government's *Excellence in Cities* programme, the building was restored and extended. Commissioned by the Learning Trust (the body responsible for education in Hackney) and UK Online, Brady Mallalieu Architects created a new flexible educational space to the rear of the portico. The drama of the open colonnades was maintained by ensuring that the extension is invisible from Linscott Road. Once found, the addition adopts a modern style, clearly distinguishable from the historic fragment. The new building provides classrooms, meeting rooms and a café, and is protected from the glare of the sun by a huge screen of aluminium louvres. This long-standing feature on the 'Buildings at Risk' register has once again become a useful space, where children (and adults) can learn new computer skills to improve their life chances. Andrew Reed would surely have approved.

Above: Front elevation of the Salvation Army Congress Hall, 1967.

Left: New aluminium louvres of the extension juxtaposed against the lofty Greek Doric columns of the dramatic portico, 2005.

Patrick Lynch

Hackney Empire

Mare Street E8

Architect Frank Matcham 1901 | restoration Tim Ronalds Architects 2004 | listed Grade II

A Place for Us

Frank Matcham fulfils the Canadian novelist William Robertson Davies' description of an 'egoist'. Unlike an 'egotist' – who always assumes that they are right – the 'egoist' stands for the best values of their art form and aspires to do what is right. Davies' masterpiece *The Deptford Trilogy* juxtaposes 20th-century Jungian psychoanalysis with 19th-century theatrical impresarios via the privileged world of modern Toronto and small-town manners of fictional Deptford. He brilliantly situates the problems that beset the modern mind when it attempts to grapple with its own past and to wrest meaning from this encounter. His egoist is Sir John Tresize, a thinly disguised analogue of Henry Irving, the great Victorian 'actor-manager'. Sir John is described as "the last of a kind that has now vanished" and "wholly devoted to an ideal of theatrical art that was contained – so far as he was concerned – within

himself". Davies distinguishes him from 'The egotist' who is "all surface; underneath is a pulpy mess of self-doubt." In contrast an egoist, like Sir John, is a much more serious being, who makes himself, his instincts, yearnings and tastes the touchstone of every experience. The world truly is his creation. I can't help thinking of Matcham in these terms.

Frank Matcham belonged to a world of self-made men driven by hard work towards a vocation, able to convert craft into art via their great ingenuity, tenacity and brilliant powers of concentration. He was a modern man used to the extreme situations of the modern metropolis, able to combine practical thinking with an ornate imagination. Respect for the past didn't get in the way of innovation in his world view, and their reconciliation is evident in his theatre designs. Matcham was an eclectic designer, mixing Roman, Egyptian, Greek and Islamic details together – in a

Far left: Exterior with the bold lettering of the extension by Tim Ronalds Architects.

Above: Stage showing curtain by Dutch designer Petra Blaisse, 2004.

63

satisfying stew of references and visual jokes. He happily used historical tropes to solve modern problems. Loggia are converted into balconies, arenas into steadily oscillating wings of seating raked surely but gently beneath arcaded galleries and pseudo-Byzantine domes. The Hackney Empire theatre was thrown up in just 38 weeks from his initial commission. And yet in this period of feverish activity he was working on at least two other theatres, and somehow he managed to make a coherent and nuanced work while creating an ideal environment for viewing music hall revues. The interior is a perfect example of arranged ellipses staggered in plan and section to create the optimum sight-lines for spectators. A circle is implied but only completed when an actor takes the stage. He echoes the circle in his declamations, sending it back to us as voice projection. Words and music complete the architectural experience, complementing visual harmony with sound and light. The manic energy required to create the brilliant interiors of the Hackney Empire is a sort of practical magic akin to showmanship. The multiple entrances and fire exits and stacked layers of tiered seating do not simply represent a class-bound society but the practical genius of a man operating, just as the fictional Tresize was, in an age where "there was no Arts Council to keep him afloat when he failed, or to pick up the bill for an artistic experiment, or act of daring".

Yet for all this brio, the Hackney Empire was a hemmed-in world, secreted behind the street on cheap land, with only a theatrical portico slapped on its face like grease paint. In 2004, the task facing Tim Ronalds was not only to restore but also to elaborate upon the architectural situation, with funds from the Arts Council, Heritage Lottery Fund and Sir Alan Sugar; not to create an alternative world but to make the theatre part of the world. Ronalds opens the theatre to the street, turning it around the corner to the modern setting of the Technology Learning Centre and the art-deco Hackney Town Hall and its piazza. The Samuel Pepys' public house used to sit where the new Marie Lloyd theatre bar is now.

The new development brought with it a new square and the opportunity for the new bar to spill out into this space, uniting street life with local government, the arts, education and heritage. Ronalds cannily recognised that the internalised world of Matcham's auditorium needed little major doing with it, and that the two new buildings should complete and extend the volume of the old theatre, providing modern technical facilities and enabling the existing theatre to work well for today's drama companies. The fly tower is an elegant and simple translucent glass block,

demurely sat at the back, merging with the hinterland of industrial buildings, and reflecting the sky and blending in with it. In contrast, the new addition facing Mare Street and the square extends the buff tone of the moulded terracotta of the old flank façade, translating its flatness into a spatial figure somewhere between sign and sculpture. Public rooms for weddings and council meetings occupy the new corner, uniting the theatricality of peoples' lives with the various sacred games of art and government, emphasising the various performances of *Homo Ludens*.

Massive terracotta letters hang from the slenderest of steel brackets like a conjuror's trick. The rugged corner hovers above a slick glass wall that slides open to allow drinkers to enjoy the piazza. This spatial and temporal dynamism somehow supports the lettering above. Yet this paradox, of heaviness set above something so thin that it even slides away, works well though it breaks with architectural convention. A simple white glass canopy defines an illuminated threshold and hangs like a ribbon between street and building, defining an edge that is fluid and open to the flow of crowds. Perhaps this amazing spatial generosity and openness is Ronalds' gift to Matcham? His admiration for his predecessor's talent is mingled with an astute sense of the inherent humour in theatre design, and Ronalds is not scared of telling a structural lie in order to reveal an architectural truth. The towering text hovers magically above a busy public space like a curtain that has been lifted between the theatre and the stage. In this gesture of inversion the street becomes the stage, and the theatricality of public life is recovered for us.

Petra Blaisse's wonderful textiles add another layer to this dramatic narrative, deepening and amplifying the threshold between theatre and everyday life. Part tapestry and part screen, gorgeous gauze and lustrous velvet combine to echo the essential character of the collaboration between the two architects. While most modern architects cannot resist treating their Victorian antecedents as pompous and uptight while behaving like buffoons themselves, Ronalds delights in playing the straight man to Matcham's jester. The Victorian is revealed as an architect of wafer-thin effects and effervescent screens, and the modern architect is happy to add weight and dignity to his grandfather's jubilant fun. I love this combination. If anything, Ronalds has improved Matcham's building for him, bringing it up to date for the world today with skill and empathy, joyful energy and careful exuberance. Like all the best duos, the quiet one manages to disguise how hard he is working to enable the egoist to shine forth. Bravo!

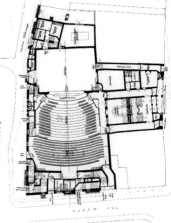

Above: Original plan by Frank Matcham, 1899.

Far left: Gilded plasterwork.

Margaret Willes

London Fields Lido

London Fields E8

Architect H A Rowbotham and T L Smithson 1932 | restoration S&P Architects 2006

One of the greatest pleasures in life is to discover that something thought lost forever is back, and in a much-improved incarnation. This is my feeling about the open-air bathing pool in London Fields. In 1982, I moved into nearby Appleby Road, and discovered the pool, swimming there a few times before it closed in 1988, apparently for good. Now it is back, with heated water and comfortable facilities.

A lido for London Fields was first mooted in February 1928 when government funds were available as compensation for appropriating land on Hackney Marshes to build a munitions factory during the First World War. London County Council (LCC) offered to provide the pool on condition that the costs would not exceed £10,000, and that Hackney Borough Council would shoulder half the costs of construction and maintenance. This was a period of great enthusiasm for open-air swimming, and nowhere

was it more popular than in London. The tradition can be traced back at least to the 18th century when Clerkenwell, for example, could offer a 'Peerless Pool'. This remarkable institution was a pond that was converted into a public swimming pool by an enterprising jeweller, William Kemp, in 1743. It provided all kinds of amenities, including an artificial canal stocked with fish for anglers, a small library and a bowling green. What modern swimming pool could top that?

London Fields was the ninth lido to be provided by the LCC, twinned with a pool of similar dimensions in Kennington. The likely architects were H A Rowbotham and T L Smithson who worked in the LCC Parks Department, creating a blueprint which could be followed by a construction company. In this case the pool and buildings were installed by the City Construction Company Ltd, with the operating system from the Turn-over Filter Company.

Far left: Restored lido by S&P Architects, 2006.

Above: The lido on a hot summer's day pre-restoration, 1984.

Work was completed by the late spring of 1932, and the excitement of the opening was captured by reports in the *Hackney Gazette*. A certain amount of heavy-handed humour surrounded a suggestion that either the Mayor of Hackney or the chairman of the Parks and Open Spaces Committee should take a dip during the opening ceremony – a precedent set thirty years earlier at the inauguration of Haggerston Baths, which were indoor and heated. In the event, the Mayor pleaded a bad cold when the public opening took place in London Fields on Saturday 30 April 1932. The *Gazette* called the Lido "the last word in up-to-date bathing pools", explaining that it was "designed to trap all the sunshine the summer may see fit to yield, and its mellow brickwork, bright red roofing and handsome cubicles give it a very cheerful appearance".

The *Gazette* was not indulging in hyperbole when describing London Fields as up-to-date. The design represented a new approach to pool design with the changing rooms housed in identical ranges, each with a central brick pavilion flanked by arcades of wooden cubicles. This offered ample facilities for groups and individuals, together with a first aid room. At the northern end a sun-bathing terrace was provided, together with a refreshment kiosk, and a green-tiled aerator that was connected to the filtration system. At the opening the raising of a red flag marked the starting of this filtration plant, followed by a display of swimming and high diving by Miss Agnes Nicks – a long-distance champion. Thereafter, the crowd of local inhabitants that had gathered were allowed to swim, and many were braver than the Mayor.

Unusually, the Lido was closed throughout the Second World War, but reopened after extensive restoration in 1951. For my neighbours in Appleby Road, it represented the summer equivalent of the *Palais de Dance*: a place where they would hold family reunions, with the young meeting their friends and conducting romances, while the older members looked after the children. I was shown home-movies of the families ensconced in 'their patch' on the sun terrace, intercut with that other

Above: Before the restoration, 1998.

summer activity for East London, the annual pilgrimage to Kent to pick hops. On my visits to the baths, I would be invited onto their patch.

However, I confess to using the pool only in hot weather, and therefore part of a growing problem for the Lido. Less-hardy generations could not cope with the cold water during much of the year. This imbalance in use may have led to the Lido's demise in 1988, but affection for the pool continued unabated with local residents mounting a campaign to have it reopened. In 1997 a mass clean-up was organised with lorry loads of buddleia bushes and other weeds removed from the site. The following year a similar event was held to paint the most-damaged woodwork, to clear away the corrugated iron fencing and to install a banner reminding the world that the Lido was still with us.

London Fields Lido gets no mention in Pevsner, nor strangely in some other books specifically about swimming pools. This is remarkable for it has one important distinction: the size of the bathing area when built was 165 feet by 66 feet. The 'Olympic' scale was one of the arguments put forward by the London Fields User Group for the restoration of the pool, and in 2004 Hackney Council was persuaded. Even as S&P Architects, specialists in sports architecture and community swimming projects, drew up a feasibility plan, a fire destroyed some of the changing rooms. However, the Council's resolution remained firm, and a scheme was adopted for a 50 metre by 17 metre deck-level pool, reducing the original depth to a maximum of two metres. The colourful appearance noted by the *Hackney Gazette* in 1932 has been recaptured by multi-coloured lockers intermingled with the individual cubicles, while refreshments are offered not in the original kiosk, but from a shop serving both users of the pool and visitors. London Fields Lido was duly reopened in 2006, with the water heated by highly efficient gas condensing boilers, so that bathers can enjoy the wonderful experience of swimming through clouds of steam on wintry mornings.

Laurie Elks

The Round Chapel

(formerly Clapton Park United Reformed Church)

Glenarm Road E5

Architect Henry Fuller 1869-71 | restoration Cazenove Architects 1991-3 | listed Grade II*

The Clapton Park United Reformed Church was constructed in 1869-71 for the congregation that had outgrown its existing place of worship at the Old Gravel Pit Chapel in Morning Lane. The new church served the growing population of Lower Clapton, which consisted of a respectable Pooteresque community of clerks, tradesmen and professional people.

The architect, Henry Fuller, rejected the traditional nonconformist rectangular 'preaching box'. The Church included a horseshoe-shaped space for worship, with a highly original combination of Classical and Gothic features (with a decidedly Romanesque external aspect). The elegant use of structural iron pillars and the complete dispensation with the traditional nave and aisle pattern make this vast soaring space a wonder to behold.

The design was innovative, confident and controversial. A contemporary issue of *Building*

News praised Fuller's attempt to find a new direction for nonconformist architecture, but other journals considered that the design was not appropriate for a church. A Sunday school was subsequently added on an adjoining site in Powerscroft Road, incorporating a large suite of rooms and facilities to serve the diverse activities of the church community.

The Church fell on hard times after the Second World War, with the decline of religious observance and the departure of much of the community to the outer suburbs. By the 1990s church membership had fallen to 12 people, and worship was transferred to the Sunday school, leaving the main space unused and unheated. With mounting structural problems, including rampant dry rot and a dilapidated roof, church activities – such as the Sunday school and youth group – progressively ceased, leaving the entire building grossly under-used.

Above: Exterior of the Clapton Park United Reformed Church, 1966.

The Church elders considered a number of options for the building, including conversion into flats, or demolition followed by redevelopment that would have incorporated a church on a much smaller footprint. There was precedent for the latter solution, as the United Reformed Church had done this at other churches in Rectory Road and Manor Road in Stoke Newington[1]. The development proposals were rejected by English Heritage and Hackney Council following objections from Hackney Historic Buildings Trust, the Hackney Society and others. The listing of the Round Chapel, on account of its use of cast iron pillars and innovative interior, was upgraded from Grade II to II*, with specific mention of the merit of the interior.

Following this, the Trust collaborated with English Heritage to identify a viable future for the building. Emergency repair works were carried out from 1991-3. Funded by English Heritage with support from Hackney Council, the roof structure, which was on the verge of collapse, was stabilised and the dry rot was eradicated. Meanwhile, studies were commissioned to explore the viability of developing the building as a space for the performing arts – possibly as part of Hackney Council's strategy to develop a 'cultural quarter' alongside Sutton House, Hackney Empire and the Central Methodist Hall (later to become Ocean).

There followed a complex tripartite negotiation between the Trust, the Church and English Heritage whereby it was agreed that the Trust would take over the main space (plus a small suite of adjoining rooms) for the sum of £1. The quid pro quo was that the Church would receive funding to restore the Sunday school, as well as being freed from the millstone of caring for a historic building. The main space was restored by Cazenove Architects; and the Sunday school was restored by Terry Dacombe, an architect and member of the United Reformed Church.

For the Church, there was a happy conjunction between the restoration of the retained parts and the arrival of an inspiring minister, Doug Gay. Energetic and entrepreneurial new congregants broadened the social and ethnic make-up of the Church community, set up community outreach initiatives, and exploited the revamped premises by hiring out the venue for events.

For its part, the Trust succeeded in attracting a variety of individuals and groups to use its beautifully restored building. The Round Chapel has played host to weddings and funerals, concerts (including *Oasis* and *Coldplay*), television productions (including *The Lost World* and *Question Time*), ceilidhs, Turkish concerts, the annual Hackney Schools Music Festival and tai chi.

However, the use of the Round Chapel as a space for the performing arts has not been without problems. While the Victorian appearance of the building has been restored, the work did not extend to restoration of the under-floor heating system, nor to resolving the excessively 'bright' acoustic. Additionally, the division of the building has left the main space lacking adequate ancillary areas, with only very limited toilet, kitchen and meeting facilities. Various arts organisations have considered establishing themselves at the Round Chapel, but have been deterred by the cost of overcoming these difficulties. Since 2005 Christian Life City (an evangelical church) has made the Round Chapel its home, sharing the building with other users. The income from this church has stabilised the Trust's finances, but has not as yet provided the necessary funds for an effective heating system. It is perhaps fair to say that while the Round Chapel has still not fully realised its potential as an artistic and cultural centre, it has amply demonstrated itself as an effective community resource – 'the largest village hall in Hackney'.

Above right: Rampant dry rot, 1987.

Far left: Interior of the church showing the pews that were destroyed, c.1910.

Nick Holder

St Augustine's Tower

The Narroway, Mare Street E8

Architect unknown century | rebuilt 1510s | restoration Albert Powys 1931-2;
Butler Hegarty Architects 1982; Nick Alexander 2005-6 | listed Grade I

St Augustine's Tower is Hackney's oldest surviving building, and it is also something of an icon of the modern London borough, appearing, for example, in the official coat-of-arms and as a mast-head for the *Hackney Gazette*. Like many of Hackney's old buildings it had been ignored, although it was never quite forgotten. The tower is all that remains of the medieval parish church of St Augustine's, the majority of which was demolished in 1798 when the new church of St John-at-Hackney was built. The tower was originally retained as a separate bell-tower because the new church didn't have a bell-tower until 1814 (and it wasn't until 1854 that the bells from St Augustine's were finally transferred to St John's). Unusually, the tower was situated at the south-west corner of the medieval church, which used to extend eastwards over what is now the grass of the churchyard (medieval church towers are usually built at the end of the nave rather than an aisle).

After the 'rediscovery' of all things medieval in the 19th century, the first restoration of the tower took place towards the end of the century when several of the windows were rebuilt in the original style.

In 1931-2 Albert Powys of the Society for the Preservation of Ancient Buildings (SPAB) restored the tower for Hackney Council – who had purchased it for £5. SPAB repaired the buttresses, restored the windows and completely rebuilt the parapets. In 1982 Butler Hegarty Architects repaired the doors, the clock and the roof. Since 1990 the tower has been looked after by Hackney Historic Buildings Trust, who secured funding for the most recent restoration in 2005-6. Nick Alexander made the tower ready for public access by weather-proofing the openings, installing electricity, repairing the stairs and fitting an electric winding mechanism to help preserve the rare 17th-century clock.

Above: Arch and doorway of the south aisle, which originally would have led from the church into the tower, 2009.

Far left: Exterior view from south-east, 1930.

An interesting story – dare I say myth – has grown up about the origin of the church: it is sometimes said that it was built or rebuilt by the medieval order of crusading monks, the Knights Templar, and that it passed to their successors, the Knights Hospitaller, in the 14th century. In fact there is remarkably little evidence for either of these assertions. Both Christian military orders did own property in Hackney, but this seems to have been a mansion, a few tenements, a watermill and some fields. Furthermore, if either of them had owned the church they would have probably held the 'advowson' or the right to appoint the rector, but this was always done by the Bishop of London. It seems more likely that the church evolved gradually, in a way that is typical of many London and Middlesex churches. It could well have been founded in the 12th century as the population of the village of Hackney grew more numerous and wealthy. New parts were probably added to the church between the 13th and the 15th centuries – perhaps a new chancel at the east end and aisles on either side of the original nave – as wealthy residents who had made money in London included bequests to their parish church in their wills. Old engravings and paintings illustrate a late medieval church with windows of the Perpendicular style, most of which seem to date to the late 15th or early 16th centuries. This is almost certainly the work of the well-connected rector Christopher Urswick and the royal accountant Sir John Heron in the 1510s: Heron demonstrated his generosity by placing his coat-of-arms between each arch of the nave. What we are less clear about is just how much of the church they rebuilt and how much of the earlier fabric they retained.

Let us now turn to the evidence of the tower itself. The surviving tower, which stands nearly 85 feet high (25.8 metres), probably has two different phases of construction. As you look at the arch that leads into the tower, it is clear that the wall surrounding the arch is much less regular than the well-squared stones of the tower itself (nor does this lower part of the wall look the same as the internal faces of the tower). The arch (perhaps built in Magnesian limestone dolomite from Yorkshire) is probably slightly earlier than the rest of the tower. The whole lower face must have been the inside wall of the south aisle, probably built in the 15th century. The stonework of the main body of the tower is quite different. It is often described as Kentish ragstone, but the external walls are built in higher quality 'freestone' from Kent (from the Hythe Beds of the Lower Greensand). When you look at the best-preserved parts of the tower, where it is protected from the weather by the old town hall, you can see that the stones were originally rectangular 'ashlar' –

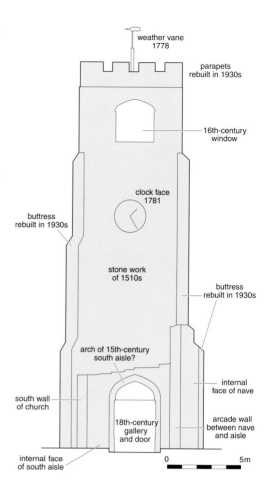

precisely cut and bonded with thin joints of lime mortar. The slightly rusticated appearance of the stones today is due to weathering. Higher up the tower there used to be string courses – slightly protruding horizontal bands of stone – fragments of which survive on the north face. The tower can therefore be seen as a prestigious and extremely expensive addition to the church that almost certainly dates to the extensive rebuilding of the 1510s by Christopher Urswick and Sir John Heron.

We should therefore imagine the tower as a new white building of the early 16th century, rising high over the church and shining in the sunlight, with faint bands dividing it into four-storeys. There was a large stained-glass window facing Mare Street at ground level, with small windows on nearly every face of the second and third floors (two of the windows are now hidden behind clock faces) and larger belfry windows on the fourth stage. The tower was capped by a 'fleche' or small spire. We might then imagine Urswick and Heron climbing to the top (if indeed it was completed before the latter's death in 1521), glancing at the towers and smoke of the City of London and walking round the parapets, looking over fields towards the small church of St Mary's Stoke Newington, the mansion of Brooke House in Clapton, the mills along the Lea, and the winding roads of Homerton High Street and Mare Street below.

Above: Weather vane, 2009.

Above right: East face of St Augustine's Tower with dates of construction, alteration and repair.

Joanna Smith

Shoreditch Town Hall

Old Street EC1

Architect Cesar A Long 1866-7; William G Hunt 1901-3; A G Cross 1905-7; C T Fulcher 1937-8
restoration Niall Phillips Architects 2004-5 | listed Grade II

With its constricted site, hard up against a railway viaduct and barely set back from Old Street, Shoreditch Town Hall is a building most often seen obliquely or glimpsed in passing. But the building, amongst the most evocative survivals of late Victorian and Edwardian municipal government in the capital, deserves closer attention. Its stone façade is a hybrid, the product of a phased construction and post-fire rebuilding. This complex building history is matched by changes in status and function. For almost a century the building served as Shoreditch's administrative centre, followed by decades of neglect and under use. But in the last ten years its fortunes have revived and its architectural grandeur has been, at least partially, restored. Today the building lives again as a venue for community, cultural and business activities.

The oldest part of the building, the larger eastern section, was constructed in 1866-7 for Shoreditch

Vestry. Originally ecclesiastical in nature, the parish vestries of London had gradually evolved into local government administrative units and were the precursors of the modern London boroughs. Shoreditch used its own vestry surveyor, Cesar A Long, to design the building. Its exterior was in a classical style, modelled on Renaissance Italian palace fronts. This was meant to evoke substance, probity and durability – hence the use of stone, but not, as vestries were notoriously cost-conscious bodies, extravagance. Internally the building had a large, ornamented room at the rear for the vestry meetings, a modest suite of offices and a grand public hall that occupied the entire first floor. This was used for lectures, concerts and other entertainments; this kind of facility being much in demand in populous districts such as Shoreditch.

The western extension was added in 1901-3, designed by William G Hunt following an

*Above: Barrel-vaulted
public hall rebuilt in
1905-7 by A G Cross, 1975.*

PROGRESS

architectural competition, and built by the Shoreditch firm, Killby and Gayford. Its construction had been necessitated by the growth of local government and by major municipal reform, which in 1900 swept away the vestries and created Metropolitan Boroughs in their place. Externally the addition respected the design of the earlier building and copied its architectural forms, the rusticated ground floor and Corinthian pilasters, but added an off-centre tower. The enhanced civic status of the Metropolitan Borough of Shoreditch was celebrated in its decoration – a torch-bearing statue of Progress on the tower and a pediment with reclining figures personifying the Council's motto 'More Light, More Power'. Within, the extension provided additional offices, committee rooms and a mayor's parlour, while the vestry room was transformed into a council chamber.

The exterior attained its present form in 1905-7, after a serious fire destroyed Long's public hall. Rebuilt by A G Cross, the new barrel-vaulted space required the addition of a curiously styled pediment on the front of the building to disguise a new roof. Lastly, the building acquired a substantial but functional rear extension in 1937-8, accessed from Rivington Street. But in 1965 administrative reforms, which merged the old Metropolitan Borough into the newly created London Borough of Hackney, resulted in a shift in the civic focus to Hackney Town Hall. The Shoreditch building was downgraded to council offices; its loss of status exacerbated by an unsympathetic refurbishment and the removal of its council chamber fittings.

By the mid 1990s the Council's occupation of the increasingly shabby building was in decline, and concerns for its future prompted its inclusion on English Heritage's 'Buildings at Risk' register. It was at this time that I first visited the town hall, as part of project to record the architecture of London's local government. Despite years of less than sympathetic treatment, the faded grandeur of its formal rooms and handsome administrative spaces still invoked a powerful sense of municipal ambition and progressiveness; and so it was Shoreditch's statue of Progress that was chosen to epitomise London's town halls for the front cover of the project publication.

After some discussion, an independent charity, the Shoreditch Town Hall Trust, was established in 1998. Its mission is to restore the building for community and commercial use. The first stage of a major programme of work has now been completed – partly funded by the Heritage Lottery Fund, European Regional Development Fund and Bridge House Trust – with a further phase of improvements planned. In 2002 I returned to Shoreditch to undertake an assessment of its commercial and industrial buildings for English Heritage. This was a story dominated by the East End furniture trade, but inevitably links with the town hall emerged. Several furniture manufacturers participated in local government, and two, Edward Gates and Nathan Moss, served successively as Shoreditch's first mayors. In 1893, the town hall was used as a venue for the Shoreditch Art Furniture Exhibition. This was intended to challenge public perceptions of East End furniture as cheap and nasty, which derived partly from the industry's identification as a non-unionised or 'sweated' trade. So, it seemed particularly fitting that the publication that emerged from the assessment was launched in Long's elegant, sensitively restored, vestry room.

Far left: Exterior with statue of Progress, 2008.

Left: Although most of its municipal functions are gone, the grandeur of the former vestry room, later council chamber, of Shoreditch Town Hall endures. Built in 1866-7, it is also the original building's most important surviving interior, 1975.

Monica Blake

Stoke Newington West Reservoir Centre

Green Lanes N4

Architects W&C French 1936 | restoration Marks Barfield Architects 2001 | listed Grade II

The Stoke Newington West Reservoir Centre is something of a miracle. First because it exists at all. Secondly because it has been imaginatively restored. In 1985 Thames Water completed the London Water Ring Main. In the same year they declared the Stoke Newington Reservoirs and filter beds to be redundant and proposed to decommission them and sell the site for development. Local residents opposed the plans and set up the Save the Stoke Newington Reservoirs and Filter Beds Campaign (generally known as Save the Reservoirs Campaign).

In addition to being a valued open space and nature reserve, the site is important in the history of London's water supply. The New River, which now terminates near the West Reservoir Centre, was created to bring fresh water to London from springs in Hertfordshire. Construction was started in 1604 by Edmund Colthurst and completed in 1613 by Sir Hugh Myddelton. Previously

Londoners had bought their water from water carriers, but once the New River had been built, they could buy clean water from the New River Company. William Chadwell Mylne constructed the Stoke Newington Reservoirs in 1830-3. The filter beds were added c.1855, following the Metropolitan Water Act of 1852 which required the filtering of domestic water supplies. Campaigners were successful in saving the West and East Reservoirs, but not the filter beds, which were developed for housing. The East Reservoir continues to play a role in supplying London's water and is a noted habitat for wildlife.

The West Reservoir Centre was built as a water filtration plant. A Modernist building of red brick with Portland stone dressings, it comprised a central tower with single-storey wings to the east and west. The walls and floors were finished in ceramic tiling and the control panels for the filtration process were of marble. The filtration

Far left: Exterior showing new east wing designed by Marks Barfield Architects and original filtration plant building, 2009.

Above: Interior of Modernist tower with remains of machinery, dials and tanks, 2009.

Above: Exterior showing former wings of the building, 1987.

plant was built by the public works contractor W&C French in 1936 to provide more rapid filtration. The primary filtration apparatus was supplied by the Paterson Engineering Company and the pumps by Gwynnes Pumps.

Hackney Council took over the filtration plant and the West Reservoir from Thames Water in 1996, and work began on conversion to a centre for watersports. Developed with the assistance of National Lottery funding, the Centre was established in 2001 and officially opened on 26 June 2003.

The restoration and refurbishment of the building was carried out by Marks Barfield Architects. Their scheme involved retention of the tower of the old building and replacement of its two wings with contemporary structures.

The tower provides a dramatic entrance space with fine views over the West Reservoir. Dials and some machinery were retained as a reminder of the building's former use, and a concrete floor slab was removed to allow views of the tanks at the top of the tower.

The artist Charlie Holmes designed two floor installations of decorative cast plates describing the attributes of water. Although the tower had been disused for almost 20 years when the scheme began, it was not derelict. Restoration involved little more than cleaning the brick and Portland stone, providing a new roof and painting the interior.

The new wings constructed of glass and steel with terracotta tile cladding on the south and side elevations replaced the original brick wings. The north elevation, which faces the water, is fully glazed. The west wing accommodates equipment stores, changing rooms and wet classrooms for sailing and kayak clubs; and the east wing is a dry area with meeting room, seminar room, environmental classroom and a café. Classrooms are well insulated and naturally ventilated.

Between the building and the water is a new hardwood deck with floating pontoons and jetties. To the west is a wooden structure serving as an external canoe store.

A year-long community consultation carried out by the Save the Reservoirs Campaign showed that local people overwhelmingly supported retention of the West Reservoir and its use for water sports and environmental activities. This has been achieved, with Greenwich Leisure Limited, on behalf of Hackney Council, offering courses for sailing, kayaking and canoeing; and the London Wildlife Trust running environmental education sessions at the East Reservoir Community Garden.

The Commission for Architecture and the Built Environment (CABE) commended the restored building for "its clarity, spatial quality and simple elegance". A plaque in the tower commemorates the Save the Reservoirs Campaign.

Paul Bolding

Sutton House

Homerton High Street E9

Architect unknown 1535 | refurbished Lionel Crane and Sydney Jeffree 1904
restoration Richard Griffiths and Julian Harrap Architects 1990-4 | listed Grade I

Sutton House is the oldest house in Hackney and one of the oldest brick houses in East London. Built in 1535, it now belongs to the National Trust, which opened it to the public in February 1994. Despite its historic importance, as recently as the 1980s its future was far from secure. The house's modern history encompasses some of the best and worst about Hackney and the National Trust.

The house, whose architect and builder are unknown, was built for Ralph Sadleir, secretary to Thomas Cromwell and later Secretary of State to Henry VIII. At the time Hackney, and particularly fashionable Homerton, was favoured by courtiers and wealthy merchants for their homes or places of retreat from the filth of the City of London.

Sadleir sold the house in 1550, preferring to live in his much grander manor house in Standon, Hertfordshire, where he died in 1587. The house,

Standon Lordship, still stands. The deed of sale referred to Sutton House just as 'the bryk place'.

The house has been much altered over time. It was built as an H-plan, three-storey brick house, with gables to the central section of the north front. It is thought these were cut back and replaced by a parapet in the 1740s. The stucco rendering of the east wing dates from the 19th century. The name 'Sutton House' was mistakenly given by the National Trust in 1953. It had been thought that the building was occupied in the early 1600s by Thomas Sutton, the founder of Charterhouse School, who in fact lived in the demolished 'Tanhouse' next door.

Substantial changes were made in 1904 by the architects Lionel Crane and Sydney Jeffree. They reunited the house (it was divided in two during the 18th century), added the Wenlock Barn and an extension on the west side of the house, which

Above: Interior showing linenfold panelling, c.1920.

81

then, as today, housed the kitchen. These changes were in the Arts and Crafts style.

In 1938 the National Trust acquired Sutton House as a result of a bequest from William Alexander Robertson in memory of his two younger brothers who fell in the First World War.

Sutton House suffered very little damage during the Second World War, but for many years after the war the house was let to a number of tenants. These included the Association of Scientific, Technical and Managerial Staffs (ASTMS) – a trade union for metal-working and transport workers. In 1982 the trade union departed and the house was left empty.

In the next few years the house was squatted, and many original features were stolen. The important linenfold panelling, that is about as old as the house, was sold to an architectural salvage company, which, when realising its importance, arranged for its return. By the mid 1980s the National Trust wanted to convert the house into flats, seeing little point in opening such a modest property. Local people felt differently and mounted a campaign to save it as a visitor attraction and an amenity for the community. The Save Sutton House Campaign (later renamed the Sutton House Society) succeeded in persuading the National Trust to restore and open the house. In 1989 Fiona Reynolds, who became Director-General of the National Trust in 2001 and a Dame in 2008, was made the first chair of the Sutton House Local Committee.

During this period a programme of conservation and restoration work was carried out first by Julian Harrap with Richard Griffiths, and subsequently by Grittiths working on his own. This work included restoring the Wenlock Barn, recarving lost fleur-de-lys panels and rehanging the linenfold panelling in the parlour – one of only three rooms of its type in the London area. The restored 130-seat barn became the building's main public space and is now used for concerts, weddings and workshops with schools.

Much of what is known about the history of Sutton House was gleaned from studying material carefully collected from under the floorboards when the house was restored in the 1990s. This ranged from lacework and ceramics to keys and printed ephemera. Holiday postcards to trade union staff must have fallen off the office noticeboard and slipped through the floorboards. Perhaps the tureen lid in pieces discoverd behind panelling had been dropped by a maid who then hid it.

In recent years, campaigners have criticised the National Trust for reducing opening hours. The Trust says this is to enable it to limit staff working time and to focus more on its very successful educational programme. The reduced hours have diminished the function of the café, envisaged by the campaigners as a place for local people to gather for a coffee or simple lunch, but it is still well used.

As throughout its history, Sutton House remains a place of change. In 2005 the National Trust acquired adjacent land that had for many years been a car breaker's yard. It plans to use the land to create a garden.

In January 2009 work started on this garden. In the first phase, the walls will be repaired using specially made bricks to match the house. In a later phase, paint on the wall of the house will be removed to reveal more of the original brick diapering. However, before the garden can be created, the land will need to be decontaminated as it is polluted by heavy metals and asbestos.

In 2007 an evaluation trench dug by the Museum of London found what could be the east wall of the 'tanhouse'. Since the land was once owned by Thomas Sutton, it is intended that the garden will reflect that link, explaining the incorrect naming of the house.

Far left: Great Chamber, c.1920.

Above: Exterior, 1985.

Forgotten

(or lost buildings)

"Buildings are big things and you might be forgiven for thinking that it must be all but impossible to lose them."

Jonathan Glancey, 'Lost Buildings' (2008)

Leafing through a copy of Elizabeth Robinson's 'Lost Hackney' (1989) is a soul-destroying experience for the building historian. This book offers a fascinating glimpse into pre-industrial Hackney, aptly described by Iain Sinclair as an "Arcadian suburb of grand houses". Unfortunately, as Robinson's powerful book demonstrates, it is very easy to lose buildings.

The following chapter, inspired by this wonderful book, seeks to highlight what has been lost since the 1960s – when the Hackney Society began.

Left: Woodberry Down Comprehensive School.

Patrick Hammill

The Atlas Works

Berkshire Road E9

Architect unknown 1863 | demolished 1989

The Atlas Works was one of the last remnants of a period when Hackney was quietly supporting science and industry. Shoreditch, being just outside the perimeter of the City, traditionally hosted businesses that the City Fathers did not want inside their walls.

The East End of London and Hackney Wick, in particular, was developed as the industrial heart of London – a place where the smelly, noisy and noxious industries could be placed down wind of the gentry thus protecting them from all those nasty factories. This industrial development was taken one stage further with the coming of the canals and railways, allowing further industries to populate the banks of the River Thames and its tributaries.

Hackney Wick sits on the River Lea and the Lee Navigation Canal, and was the ideal home to factories that could be supplied from the river,

and where their waste could be taken away by boat or simply flushed directly into the water. Hence the area could support industries that were simply too smelly, smoky or dangerous to have closer to more densely populated urban areas. Companies such as the British Xylonite Company, who invented the first plastic in the world which was called 'parkesine'; Carless, Capel and Leonard, who distilled petroleum at their Hope Chemical Works on Wallis Road, inventing in the process the word 'petrol'; and the Atlas Works on Berkshire Road contributed to the creation of London's early industrial heartland.

Built in 1863, the Atlas Works represented one of the last examples of this industrial heritage. Until demolished for housing in the late 1980s some of the original building survived while other parts were redeveloped in the 1880s. To the west was the 1863 stucco frontage, including a large stone statue of Atlas – the Titan from Greek

Far left: View south-east over the factory rooftops, showing chimney with 'Bronco' and 'Dixcel' inscriptions. The Clarnico Confectioners' works can be seen in the background, c.1966.

Above: Interior view of 'queen post' roof in the part of the factory built in 1863, c.1965.

Above: Elevation from Gainsborough Road with views of the office, warehouse and weighbridge. Gainsborough Primary School and the Trowbridge Estate can be seen in the background. Leabank Square can now be found on the site, 1984.

mythology who held up the heavens on his shoulders – that was demolished in 1983. The main building had elements of a simple Arts and Crafts style with blue brick details, a queen post roof and an interior with large span arches and fine brick arcading.

One of the earlier companies to own Atlas Works was Brooke Simpson Spiller. They had bought the company of William Henry Perkins who had discovered modern organic chemical aniline dyes in 1856, the key step in moving from natural to synthetic dyes. Brooke Simpson Spiller moved the firm from Greenford, in west London, to Hackney Wick where they employed the organic chemist, Arthur George Green, who discovered the manufactured dye Primuline, also known as 'Direct Yellow'. Green moved on to other companies and later became Professor of Colour Chemistry at Leeds University. A further discovery

at Hackney Wick was was a blue dye made by Professor Raphau Meldola and named after him, another key stage in discovering colour dyes for industry. A large collection dye-stuffs made in Hackney Wick are on display in the Powerhouse Museum in Sydney, Australia. In 1986 traces of blue and crimson dyes could be found in the brickwork of the factory.

From 1908 to 1967 the Atlas Works continued to serve the nation as the home of Bronco Ltd, 'the deluxe toilet paper' which despite their motto was the manufacturer of one of the 'hard' toilet papers, renowned for its unforgiving nature by all who used it. The signs for 'Bronco' survived after the firm left the site. Finally 'Bronco' stopped production in 1989 after England discovered the joy of soft toilet papers, and the last years of the Atlas Works were as multi-occupied small manufacturing units.

Jerry Tate

Bishopsgate Station and Goods Yard

Bethnal Green Road and Shoreditch High Street E2

Architect John Braithwaite 1839 and 1843 (Bishopsgate Station); Alfred Langley 1881 (Goods Yard)
demolished 2008, except listed structures

Standing somewhat forlornly on Shoreditch High Street the brick arches of the Braithwaite viaduct are all that is left of the original Bishopsgate Goods Yard. Currently undergoing transformation from derelict site to a rejuvenated Shoreditch Station, with new offices and housing, the site is to become a hive of construction activity as a prelude to the latest phase in the evolution of this historic area that borders the City of London.

The original station on the site was a passenger terminus for the Eastern Counties Railway Company ending the proposed line from Norwich and Great Yarmouth first conceived in 1836. The company's engineer John Braithwaite completed the initial station design in 1839, with construction starting in the same year. Braithwaite, born in 1797, was one of the pioneers of railway engineering and a contemporary of the Stephenson brothers, building some of the first steam-driven vehicles as well as associated civil engineering projects. During construction the station scheme was extended to accommodate the Northern and Eastern Railway Company, replacing a planned terminus in Islington. In 1843 the works were completed with trains running to Romford and eventually Norwich as the company merged with other companies to form the Great Eastern Railway (GER) in 1862. The station design was unusual as the platform level was raised above the street on brick arches, now the famous remaining viaduct, while the corrugated-iron roof was supported by 17 cast-iron columns. The buildings surrounding the station, designed by the architect Sancton Wood, were of an Italianate stone-faced design. Although the station was reasonably well received by the architectural and engineering press, complaints were made regarding access and overcrowding of the concourse, partly caused by the difference between platform and street levels.

Above: East side, south roadway, 1985.

When Liverpool Street Station opened in 1875 it allowed the Great Eastern Railway Company to close the Bishopsgate terminus as a passenger station and convert it into a goods yard. Completed in 1881 the goods yard was on three levels, two having rail and road access above and below the original brick viaduct with a third upper-level warehouse. Mostly completed on the original substructure, the conversion was designed by the GER's company engineer Alfred Langley. The upper-level warehouse was covered with an iron and glass roof resting on massive iron columns. Although the surrounding buildings were demolished, some Italianate detailing remained in the moulded terracotta and white brick detailing of the window surrounds. The multi-levelled goods yard relied on the latest technology to operate as wagons were shifted between levels through a series of turntables, capstans and hydraulic hoists powered by two large accumulators. The scale of the operation was vast, with up to 2,000 tons of goods being moved through the station every day. As the railway line connected to the busy Harwich to Zeebrugge ferry route the area became heavily influenced by the rich and varied imports from Europe. It is hard to imagine how this exotic produce must have impacted on the wider area of Commercial Road, even though a planned fruit and vegetable market was quashed by the nearby traders at Spitalfields.

On 5 December 1964 the upper level warehouse of the goods yard was devastated by a fire. The remains of the warehouse were removed and the station remained partly operational until 1967, when it was closed. By the 1970s all the track had been lifted and the upper platform level had become overgrown and abandoned. A variety of smaller ventures started colonising the site, ranging from temporary car parks to car breaker's yards. Despite proposals to demolish the existing structure by 1999 the brick viaduct was home to manufacturing facilities, artist studios, restaurants and even a swimming pool and gym, while the upper level accommodated a Karting track.

In March 2002 the Braithwaite Viaduct – as the brick arches had become known – were listed Grade II. Following the listing a campaign was launched by English Heritage to retain the historically important arches and incorporate a new Shoreditch Station for the extended East London Line above as well as commercial spaces below. By 2009 all of the non-listed original structures had been demolished and the site is now being planned for development by Hammerson PLC and Ballymore Properties Ltd to include the new station, planned to open in 2010, as well as a high-density mixed-use development designed by the architecture practices Foster and Partners, and Allies and Morrison. The site will find a new life as part of the improved transport infrastructure for the East End as well as home to the modern service industries which have replaced those of steam and trade.

Far left: View from corner of Shoreditch High Street, 1962.

Above: An accumulator and hoist, 1985.

Sharman Kadish

Clapton Federation Synagogue

Lea Bridge Road E5

Architect Marcus Glass 1931-2 | demolished 2006

Sha'are Shomayim (Gates of Heaven)

Clapton Federation Synagogue was the last and the only London synagogue designed by prolific Jewish architect Marcus Glass who was based in Newcastle upon Tyne.[1] Pevsner rated its sister building Sunderland Synagogue as "vigorous and decorative".[2] Glass undertook a series of synagogue commissions, both conversions and new-build projects, starting out in Newcastle, his home town, with Jesmond Synagogue (1914-5); moving on to Sunderland's Ryhope Road Synagogue (1928); and finally Clapton (1931-2). All were built for upwardly mobile immigrant communities. Today, many London Jews wrongly consider Hackney to be part of the East End – along with Whitechapel and Stepney – a poor neighbourhood from which they and their families were only too pleased to escape. However, from the end of the 19th century until the Second World War, Hackney's

rows of suburban villas were regarded as the height of lower-middle-class respectability.

Oral testimony has dated the congregation in Upper Clapton back to 1919 when a *Minyan* (the quorum of ten men required for public worship according to Orthodox Jewish law) was formed in a private house in Mount Pleasant Lane. From there it progressed to "a ramshackle house in Lea Bridge Road".[3] The site was purchased in 1921, but it was not until 25 October 1931 that the foundation stone was laid for a purpose-built synagogue 'on vacant land'[4] next door. By this time the congregation had affiliated, in 1928, to the Federation of Synagogues, the umbrella organisation founded in 1887 to succour the needs of East London congregations. The Federation made loans and encouraged the opening of 'model' synagogues, conversions and new-build, both in the East End proper and in neighbourhoods of secondary settlement, like

Far left: Exterior of Clapton Federation Synagogue, 1998.

Above: Showing Clapton Jewish Day School next door, 1966.

Hackney. The Clapton Federation Synagogue was opened on 5 June 1932, designed to accommodate 400 men and 300 women in the gallery, at a cost of £12 000.[5]

Marcus Kenneth Glass (1887-1932) was a first-generation Jewish immigrant from the Russian Empire who became a successful architect.[6] Born Yekusiel Glaz he arrived in Newcastle upon Tyne in the early 1890s.[7] He was the third of the six children of Max (or Mendel) Glaz, a tailor, and his wife Dana (née Gottlieb). The family came from Riga, the capital of Latvia. His father seemed to have prospered quickly, despite his lack of English. He acquired some property and naturalised in 1900. Little is known about Marcus's architectural education. He set up sole practice in 1914, soon interrupted by war service with the Royal Engineers. After the First World War he returned to architecture with an office in Saville Row, in Newcastle city centre. He acquired a comfortable villa (which he much improved) in Jesmond and he married Hannah Woolf at Hammersmith Synagogue in London in 1922. In 1925 he became a fellow of the RIBA.

Marcus Glass's progress from humble beginnings was rapid but was sadly cut short by his early death in January 1932 at the age of 45. He died shortly before Clapton was finished. Quantity Surveyor S Saunders took on responsibility for completing the project, which was being built by W M Brand of Stamford Hill. Glass's early death may explain why this talented architect has been largely forgotten and his work has gone unappreciated.

The synagogues at Jesmond, Sunderland and Clapton were Glass's most important works. They were stylistic triplets, differing only in matters of detail. All three possessed solid corner towers, a dominant curved gable which displayed up high the *Luhot* ('Tablets of the Law') above a starburst or sun-ray window, jolly red and yellow *Ablaq* – alternating light and dark courses of brickwork, artificial stone dressings; arcaded porches with Byzantine basket capitals, and a colourful mosaic band over the entrance porch. In the case of Clapton, the corner towers were canted with slit windows. The entrance porch had a triple arcade; the band above was of blue, turquoise and gold, and carried the Hebrew inscription "Open for me the gates of righteousness…" (from Psalm 118:19).

Inside Clapton Federation Synagogue, the delicate plasterwork Ark canopy was highly decorative, painted and gilded. It was classical in form, but featured decoration of Islamic and Byzantine origin, especially the cushion capitals to the columns and the chevron patterns on the shafts. The Ark and pulpit were identical to those at

Sunderland and at Glass's Hove Hebrew Congregation Synagogue in Holland Road (1929-30) – a converted Victorian gymnasium. All these pieces must have been made by the same craftsmen, and probably came from the same workshop in Newcastle upon Tyne.

Sunderland Synagogue, the architect himself declared, was executed in "a free Byzantine style…that it should be unmistakably a synagogue".[8] Indeed, Glass had strong views on the issue of architectural style. According to his friend C B Moses:

"On our visits together to a number of London Synagogues, Mr Glass often expressed to me his disappointment at the absence in some of them of what he termed the 'Oriental' atmosphere. He maintained that no matter in what country Jews lived, they were an Eastern race, and in the building of his Synagogues he would always give prominence to that Oriental feature."[9]

'Orientalism' held sway in synagogue architecture across Europe in the late 19th century. By the early 1930s such theories were a bit passé. However, no one could accuse Glass of being anything less than contemporary in his design work. In his hands, decorative 'Oriental' features were interpreted in a strikingly individual, cinematic Art Deco style. His predilection for bold and colourful façades enlivened the streetscape, whether in a run-down north-eastern town or an inner London suburb.

Shockingly, Clapton Federation Synagogue was demolished in 2006 in the face of local attempts by the Clapton Conservation Areas Advisory Committee to get it listed. Prior to demolition the building was systematically stripped of its interior fixtures and fittings. Sunderland Synagogue, listed Grade II in 1999, today stands abandoned, now a 'Building at Risk'. The Jewish community in this depressed Tyneside town has dwindled or moved away. Common to the cases of these two strikingly similar buildings[10] was the fact that they were both sold to property developers within the Jewish community – chastening for those of us concerned to protect Anglo-Jewry's architectural heritage.

Far left: Interior showing the Ark of the Clapton Federation Synagogue, 2005.

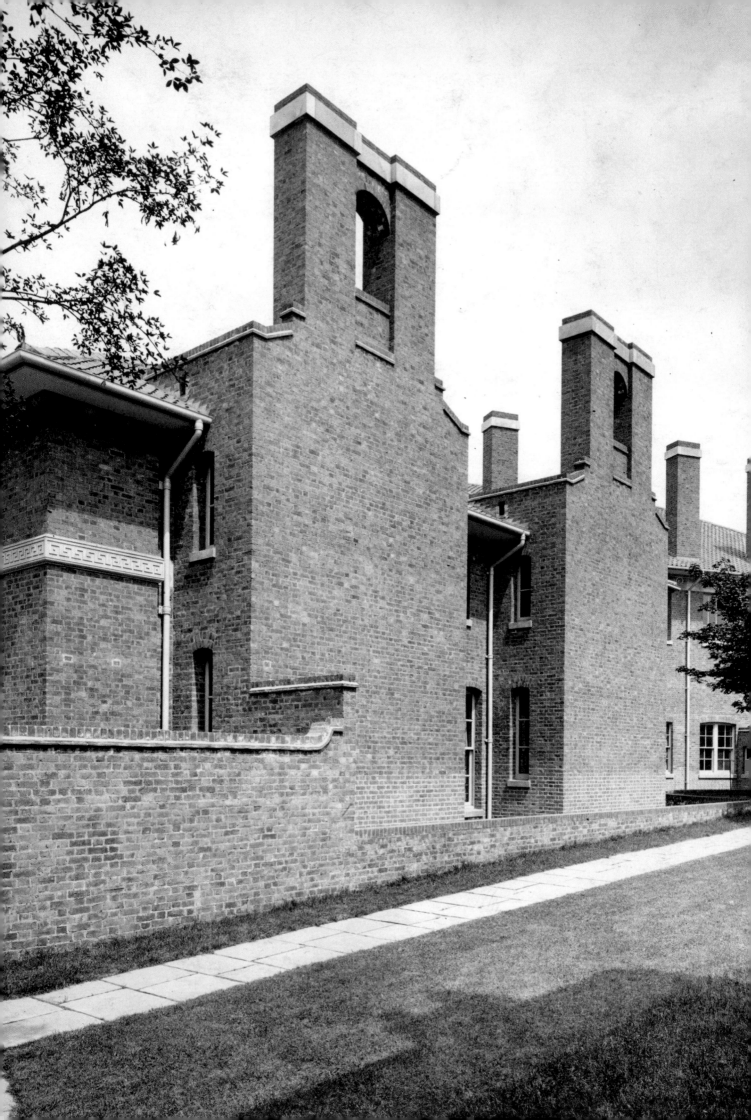

Ann Robey

Eton Manor Boys' Club

Riseholme Street E9

Architect Harry Goodhart-Rendel 1912 | demolished 1969

It is as much for its social history, as for architectural distinction that Eton Manor Boys' Club should be remembered. The magnificent clubhouse and adjacent manor house (both built in 1912) occupied a triangular site in Riseholme Street that disappeared under the elevated section of motorway known as the A12 East Cross Route, built east of Victoria Park in the early 1970s. It was demolished with little objection, save for protests about the motorway by the fledgling Hackney Society whose secretary, David Batchelder fronted a public enquiry in March 1969.[1]

In the later 19th century it was common for Oxbridge colleges and public schools to fund East End missions or settlements to help the working classes financially, ethically, practically; and to encourage the privileged to live amongst them. Eton founded their Mission to the East End in Hackney Wick on the 17 October 1880, a little before Toynbee Hall, established in 1884 by

Samuel and Henrietta Barnett. In 1898 they described what the movement's purpose was:

"A settlement is simply a means by which men or women may share themselves with their neighbours; a club-house in an industrial district, where the condition of membership is the performance of a citizen's duty; a house among the poor, where residents may make friends with the poor."[2]

Originally connected with the St Mary of Eton Mission in Gainsborough Road (now Eastway), the Eton Manor Boys' Club evolved as a separate institution just before the First World War. In 1907 two old Etonians, Gerald Wellesley (grandson of the Duke of Wellington) and Alfred Wagg (a banker with his family's firm Helbert Wagg) became active with the mission. Both men established the first Old Boys' Club in 1909, above a coal shop in Daintry Street, which was located

Far left: Side elevation showing the magnificent chimneys, 1913.

Above: Interior of gymnasium/hall, 1913.

Above: General view from the street showing the two wings of the butterfly-shaped clubhouse with its central communal facilities, 1913.

just off the Eastway. Wellesley hoped that it would allow young men who had joined the original boys' club at the mission to remain in a club environment into adulthood, thus avoiding the evils of drink, gambling and 'street loafing'. Male unemployment was particularly high in Hackney Wick and many were supported by their wives and children who worked in local factories.[3] The Old Boys' Club soon outgrew its original clubhouse and a new building was needed. Edward Cadogan and Arthur Villiers helped Wellesley and Wagg fundraise, and soon they were able to purchase the derelict Manor Farm in Riseholme Street and employ an architect. The boys' clubs separated from the Eton Mission in 1913, after disagreements about money, the desire to play sport on Sundays, and what Wellesley described as "too much parson"!

Harry Goodhart-Rendel (1887-1959) designed the new 'butterfly-shaped' clubhouse, comprising two wings with central communal facilities. This 'butterfly' design was much favoured by Arts and Crafts architects such as Edwin Lutyens and Detmar Jellings Blow – who in 1906 designed Happisburgh Manor in Norfolk. The cost of building Eton Manor, including architect's fees and

furnishings (many designed by the architect), was £16,000, while the land cost £2,000. It was one of Goodhart-Rendel's earliest commissions and described as "very clever and very hospitable and home-like, just what is needed."[4]

The club opened in July 1913, one part housed the Boys' Club for those aged 14 to 18, and the other part contained two clubs for Old Boys. Between the wings was a large hall with a stage for dramatic performances and concerts, which was also used as a gymnasium. In the basement was a library, canteen and a shooting range. In the clubs were billiard and club rooms, bathrooms and bars serving non-alcoholic drinks. Activities ranged from debating to table tennis and boxing to first-aid. There was also a savings bank and a dentist.

The clubhouse was steel-framed and built in golden stock bricks with Portland stone dressings. The fine lettering and Greek key patterns were sculpted by Esmond Burton. The roof covering was red pantiles. Inside, the spacious rooms were painted in light buffs and greys, with white ceilings and grey woodwork. The large chimney pieces were made of red Daneshill bricks. The adjacent eight-bedroomed Manor House had beautiful

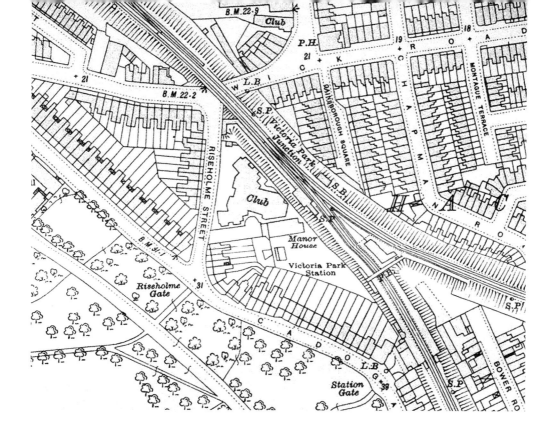

gardens with herbaceous borders and lawns for deck tennis. It was here that the Old Etonians stayed when visiting. In 1914, Gertrude Jekyll was working at Goodhart-Rendel's newly inherited estate at Hatchlands Park in Surrey and perhaps she influenced the design of the gardens at Hackney Wick. In the 1930s they were replanted and given a 'moderne' look. Out went 'Jekyll' style, replaced by flat lawns and new features including a giant chessboard and semi-circular concrete benches.

The club was barely open when the First World War broke out. Alfred Wagg kept the club going when Wellesley, Villiers and Cadogan were at war, sending parcels to the 'boys' in the trenches, supporting the injured and keeping the club open for those on leave. In 1922, Wagg moved to Surrey (where he established the Isle of Thorns Boys Camp in 160 acres, where 200 boys at a time could take country holidays) and the day-to-day management of the club passed to Arthur Villiers. It soon became the centre of his world outside his working life as a director of Barings Bank. He was strongly influenced by the philanthropic interests of his mother, Lady Jersey.

In 1923 the club bought 30 acres of wasteland over the River Lea in Leyton – which was renamed the Wilderness and turned into a fine recreation ground for club members, with numerous facilities, buildings and even a 'plunge' pool. There were squash courts, a bowling green, nine football and two rugby pitches, a cricket ground, and a running track on which the asphalt from the 1948 Olympic Stadium was re-laid. The first floodlit athletics meeting in England was held there in 1951. The best facilities were matched by the finest coaches,

including Alf Ramsey who coached the football teams before leading the 1966 England team to World Cup glory. The club was noted for its gymnastics prowess in the 1940s. Eton Manor even produced three Olympic medallists in boxing – Harry Mallin (who won two golds), Fred Grace and Nicky Gargano.

Villiers eventually built himself a modest house on the Wilderness. For several generations, Eton Manor Boys' Club was at the centre of many Hackney and Leyton men's lives. Villiers' fortune, like his leisure time, was devoted to charitable purposes. During the Second World War he campaigned for improved pensions for wounded ex-servicemen and for years helped to house, educate and obtain positions for hundreds of old boys.

But although the personal actions, involvement and financial support of Arthur Villiers were central to the expansion and running of Eton Manor Boys' Club, they were also its downfall. In 1967 Villiers made an autocratic action that devastated the lives of many: he sacked the staff and closed the club without ever explaining why. He also stopped speaking to anyone associated with the club and died in his small house on the Wilderness in 1969 at the age of 86.

Today almost everything associated with the Eton Manor Boys' Club has gone. The clubhouse was demolished for the A-road in the late 1960s, the buildings in the Wilderness went soon afterwards and the Manor Garden Allotments were flattened in 2007 in preparation for the 2012 Olympic Games, despite the allotments being bequeathed 'in perpetuity' to the plot holders, by Villiers in 1969.

Above: Ordnance Survey map. 1915.

Matt Payne

Hackney Stadium

Waterden Road E9

Architect unknown 1932 | demolished 2003

'**M**ake it a date, Friday at eight' – so went the tagline in its 1930s heyday, when Hackney Stadium drew large crowds to the industrial wastes of Hackney Wick to revel in the spectacle of motorcycle speedway – frantic races in which teams of riders would hurtle around the oval-shaped track on brakeless, souped-up motorbikes. The stadium in Waterden Road had originally started out, in 1932, as a greyhound track. The well-known cinema architect Clifford A Aish drew up a set of proposed plans, but there is no evidence that his plans were approved and used as the final designs for the building. Architecturally the stadium was a basic affair, the only pre-requisite being for form to follow function. It consisted of two brick stands either side of a 430-metre circuit, with long straights and an imposing black-and-white tote board in the centre of the track's northern bank. A shorter track inside the dog track would later accommodate speedway.

Greyhound racing had become popular in America in the 1920s and quickly caught the imagination of Britain's working classes – looking for entertainment, banter and the chance to make a few bob. The tracks were the gin palaces of their day, and Hackney soon joined the ranks of Wimbledon and Walthamstow, offering cheap, accessible thrills to the common man in the street. It was big business, and attendances across the country by the end of the 1930s totalled in the region of 17 million. The stadium cast an earthy glamour over the warehouses and chimneys of Hackney Wick, offering a refuge from work. Whether it was the shouts of the bookmakers and whining of the dogs in the traps, or the smell of methanol and roar of the bike engines, this was gritty, East End entertainment at its finest.

Over the decades, the stadium continued to draw the punters, although numbers had begun to decline from the end of the Second World War.

Far left: The Sunday market at the former Hackney Stadium, 2003.

Above: The disused track, stadium and tote board, 2001.

By the early 1990s, the outlook for many tracks, including Hackney, was bleak. Greyhound racing was simply not as popular any more and Speedway attendances had also started to wane. The track that hosted a succession of racing teams from the Hackney Wolves in the 1930s to the Kestrels in the 1980s, and had been the running ground for thousands of prized greyhounds, was itself on its last legs. The owners' dreams of building a super-stadium to take greyhound racing into the new millennium were short lived and, although investment was found to build a new multi-million pound stand in 1995, the venture was a white elephant and the company went into receivership on its opening night.

Regular punters lamented the atmosphere of the old Hackney Stadium. Greyhound commentator and broadcaster, Darrell Williams described the scene from a visit in the early 1990s:

"Hackney was no great looker. It was cheap, cheerful and gave the impression it had probably looked exactly the same back in the '60s. It was a documentary maker's dream, full of characters, old men in caps, many who had probably been coming to the track every Saturday since the year dot, and nearly all puffing away, almost as if it was a pre-requisite to attend."

The new, soulless glass monolith of the new stadium was simply no match and attendances fell further. Although the London Stadium, as it had come to be known, had fared better than Hackney's only other dog track, Clapton Stadium, which was demolished to make way for the Millfields Housing Estate in 1974, just 15 months

Above: The 'functional' stadium, 2001.

later, in December 1997, the death knell finally rang for Hackney Stadium. The doors closed, and 65 years of greyhound racing and Speedway came to an end.

With the passing of the dogs and the bikes, new life began in the decaying shell of the modern Hackney Stadium in the form of the Hackney Wick Sunday market. Week after week, the site played host to swarms of artistic types, immigrants and people on the margins of society who would come together with traditional Cockneys to trade their wares in the shadow of the old 1930s tote board, which still stood forlornly as a reminder of a bygone era. For over fifteen years, the market played out on the graveyard of the former Hackney Stadium, but by the turn of the millennium regeneration beckoned. In 1997, a failed planning application for a multi-use leisure facility – including a nightclub and cinema – was turned down over the lack of appropriate infrastructure. This paved the way for the London Development Agency (LDA) to purchase the site in 2003, razing to the ground what was left shortly afterwards.

Even at this stage, greyhound racing and Speedway fans had not given up hope that a new stadium would one day return to Hackney Wick. However, the final nail in the coffin came in 2005, with London's successful bid to host the 2012 Olympic Games. The site of the former stadium became the Olympic Media Centre, which will be converted for business use as part of the Legacy proposals. It is almost impossible to think that greyhound racing or Speedway will ever return to this particular corner of London.

Ken Worpole

The Mothers' Hospital

Lower Clapton Road E5

Architect unknown c.1840 and Alexander Gordon 1914 | demolished c.1987

Like many others conceived in East London during the Second World War, I was born in a castle: Willersley Castle, near Matlock, Derbyshire. This grand building – though infested with mice according to my mother – was commandeered by the Mothers' Hospital in Hackney between 1940-6 as part of the civilian evacuation of London, particularly of children and young mothers.

The Mothers' Hospital in Lower Clapton Road was part of an extensive network of social provision provided by the Salvation Army in Hackney from the late 19th century until the present day.

The large maternity hospital, formerly a home for unmarried women, was opened in 1913 by Queen Victoria's daughter, Princess Louise, and finally closed in 1986, having registered 123 909 live births during its operation, including our own children: one born in 1969, and the other in 1971.

The hospital occupied a prominent frontage in Lower Clapton Road with a pillared entrance gate, and two distinctive arches leading to and from the main hospital grounds at the rear. Originally it had been built to serve the poor in Hackney, though after the Second World War it was incorporated into the National Health Service. The Mothers' Hospital retained its distinctive religious identity long after, as my wife soon discovered, when hymns were sung in the wards on a Sunday evening, and sermons offered.

In many other ways it was very 'old school', though this was as much a reflection of the era as of the religious – indeed missionary – ethos of the hospital itself: fathers were discouraged from visiting for too long, or even holding the baby for fear of 'germs', let alone attending the birth. At nights some babies were wheeled in their tubular steel cots into the bathroom, where they spent the night away from their mothers, whether they cried or not.

Above: Alexander Gordon's proposed scheme for the Mothers' Hospital, 1928.

Yet the low-rise, chalet-style layout of the ward buildings helped create more of a cottage hospital effect than was evident at the other Hackney hospitals. There was also extensive tree planting in the grounds which, according to another friend whose children were born there in springtime, were full of blossom and cheerful as anything. Our two were born in winter months, alas, and my memories of both births involved trudging in the rain or snow across Hackney Downs at dusk, to catch official visiting hours. My wife obviously had the harder time, and shortly after our second child was born, she and other mothers launched a campaign for the improvement of maternity facilities in the borough, a community initiative which brought some success.

Architecturally, the Mothers' Hospital was a mixture of styles. The frontage was not purpose-built but consisted of a gap-toothed row of early Victorian houses, behind which a 2.75-acre site was used to develop six bungalow wards and an isolation block. The six 'cottage' blocks, as they were also called, were connected by a colonnade to the entrance building. Trees, shrubs and flowers were planted between the buildings, and at the far end was an ornamental garden. Ground floor plans of a typical bungalow ward show a six-bed ward, a four-bed ward and a two-bed ward serviced by a ward kitchen, toilets and bathrooms, in addition to the labour room. The wards were designed to "face north and south, thus ensuring that they shall, during the larger part of the day, receive full benefit of any sunshine that may be available". Originally the different wards were designated for different groups of mothers: married, unmarried, and one "it is hoped, to be

used by Jewess mothers, for whom we should have special arrangements made".

Neither the original architect of the scheme, Alexander Gordon FSI, LRIBA (with medical expertise provided by Dr Donald Mackintosh of Glasgow's Western Infirmary), nor the Salvation Army, were ever satisfied with the improvised frontage, however, and tried continually to raise funds to demolish the early Victorian houses and build something more imposing in their place. In the annual report of 1936, opposite a photograph of the existing hospital façade, it is stated that:

"Here is the Hospital's shabby, inadequate façade. We are sorry to see it, and none of our well-wishers will look upon it with pleasure. These drab mid-Victorian [sic] houses were adapted as a makeshift when the Hospital was built."

They had a 'dream frontage' in mind, one shown in an aerial artistic impression by Gordon himself, c.1928, which shows a five-storey monolith, a huge brick tabernacle in the Frank Lloyd Wright/Chicago style, behind which the garden bungalows appear to belong to a different world altogether.

This grand new building was never to be, though the Mothers' Hospital added a distinctive presence to Lower Clapton Road for nearly a century. When the hospital was incorporated into the National Health Service in 1948, the bold lettering on the front of the building was changed from THE SALVATION ARMY: THE MOTHERS' HOSPITAL to THE MOTHERS' HOSPITAL (SALVATION ARMY). Today the memory of its place in Hackney's history is retained in the name of the new housing development: The Mothers' Square.

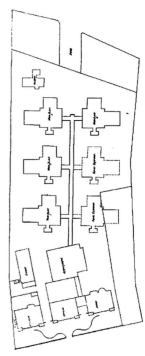

Far left: Queen Victoria's daughter, Princess Louise, is due to visit the Mothers' Hospital, 1913.

Above left: Women off to Willersley Castle during the Second World War, c.1941.

Above: Ground plan showing bungalow-style cottage blocks of the Mothers' Hospital, c.1915.

Ann Robey

Nichols Square

off Hackney Road E2

Architect John Henry Taylor 1841 | demolished 1963

By the 1830s, house building was advancing along Hackney Road from St Leonard's Church in the west, and a number of fine terraces – some of which survive today – had been built. The Nichols family evidently thought it time to speculate and profit from the lands that they had purchased over a century before. John Nichols took possession of his land and appointed an architect to design a particularly stylish small housing estate – Nichols Square.

Located on the site now occupied by Fellows Court – an estate just off Hackney Road and Cremer Street in Haggerston – Nichols Square survived until the early 1960s. This interesting development comprised of a mix of small terraces and 'Tudor Gothic' cottages was demolished for a new housing scheme.

Until early into the 19th century the main economic activities around Hackney Road were agriculture, market gardening and the nursery production of trees, flowers and vegetables. The most famous garden in the area was run by Thomas Fairchild, whose nursery lay close to Shoreditch Park.[1] Nearby was John Allport's nursery, which survived until c.1827 and was the last of the pioneering nurseries of Shoreditch and Hoxton. It formed part of the manor of Haggerston, which had been purchased by Richard Nichols in 1720.

Nichols Square was one of the more interesting speculative developments in Hackney and had an unusual plan. It was laid out and built in 1841 to the designs of John Henry Taylor.[2] It comprised a series of terraces of flat-fronted houses of classical design with porticos that surrounded a central area laid out with two rows of semi-detached Tudor Gothic cottages with steep gables and casement windows.[3] It was an attractive example of a London 'square', but, unusually, the central

Far left: A Tudor Gothic cottage with steep gable, casement windows and elaborate porch, 1950.

Above: Nichols Square with its unusual filled-in central plot, 1945.

Above: Shoreditch Lodge, 1962.

plot was filled with 28 cottages rather than with a garden.

The simple stucco houses that surrounded the square were small with four rooms arranged over two floors above a basement. These terraces had first-floor sashes and French windows (with small top-hung inset casements) on the ground floor, with projecting cills and cast-iron honeysuckle-pattern box guards. They also all had porticos in the Tuscan order with square columns.

The semi-detached Tudor Gothic cottages were slightly more spacious, comprising six rooms arranged over two floors. At the entrance to the square was a detached lodge also built in a Tudor Gothic style. The high quality of the design was typified by the fact that the two house types had

different sorts of railings – those of the terraces had a classic design and those of the cottages had a Tudor outline. The roofs were slate and the windows had moulded architraves.

Nichols Square was named after John Bowyer Nichols (1779-1863) who, as well as being the landowner, was a well-known antiquary and editor of the *Gentleman's Magazine* and the proprietor of a very prosperous printing firm. The development survived in its full extent until *c*.1860, when the western side of the square was demolished for the construction of the North London Railway extension from Broad Street to Dalston Junction. St Chad's Church, a Grade I listed building which still stands today, was erected on part of the cleared site in 1868.

In 1898-9 when Charles Booth's researchers visited Hackney Road the resulting classification of the area on the *Maps Descriptive of London Poverty 1898-99* indicated families that were fairly comfortable on good ordinary earnings. At the time Hackney Road was described as being in the intermediate stage between a living and a shopping street. Nichols Square was reputedly "monopolised by policemen – members of the City police of the Hoxton, Bethnal Green and Whitechapel sub-divisions". By 1908 the square was labelled as 'quaint'. The decline in Hackney's social status during the first half of the 20th century resulted in many properties such as those in Nichols Square being neglected and let out on short-term leases. Despite their small size, some houses in Nichols Square were even subdivided into flats.

By 1947 a number of the properties were being used as nurses' homes and were "old and show marked signs of disrepair, have bad internal arrangement and evidence of rising and penetrating dampness". The rooms were low in height and the stairs narrow and tortuous, but due to housing shortages after the war it was proposed that improvements were made, and the houses remained occupied until the early 1960s.[4]

By 1956, the end of Nichols Square was almost in sight. The London County Council suggested "consideration might be given to rehabilitating the paired Gothic houses in the centre of the square, rather than the terraces, the former being of much greater architectural value".[5] But Shoreditch Borough Council wanted to redevelop and build much needed higher-density housing on the entire site.

By 1962 the houses were in an even worse condition – many porches were missing, and the brickwork and joinery were decayed. In 1963, Shoreditch Borough Council was accused by conservationists of "leading the way on attacks on parts of London that were well worth keeping" by proposing the "demolition of an early 19th century square of, for the East End, unusually high quality".[6]

The article stated that such cottages would fetch between £10,000 and £15,000 if they were in Chelsea, but they were in Hackney and, despite recognising the architectural importance of the square, the LCC supported Shoreditch. They said "Nichols Square is unusual and interesting from a layout aspect, but in view of its poor condition preservation is not recommended".[7] Nichols Square was demolished in 1963 by Shoreditch Borough Council as part of their comprehensive house clearance policy, despite objections from local conservationists.

Fellows Court was built on the site in 1967. The landmarks of the scheme are two 16-storey blocks. Pevsner's *The Buildings of England* states that despite "tapering piers and partly open-ground floors in an effort to add some Corbusian panache" they are "hardly a success". Nichols Square was an attractive conception, and the housing built in the centre of the square was unusual. Photographic evidence suggests that the different styles of architecture of the terraces and the Tudor Gothic cottages seemed to work well together. The demolition of Nichols Square was, as the author of *Lost Hackney* states, "one of the saddest losses of all" in Hackney.[8]

Above: Air-raid shelter in Nichols Square, 1945.

Heloise Brown

Pitfield Street Baths and Washhouses

Pitfield Street N1

Architect Henry Spalding and Alfred W S Cross 1899 | demolished 1962-3

The Pitfield Street Baths and Washhouses were part of an ambitious and successful municipal project that the Shoreditch Vestry undertook in its final years before the Metropolitan Borough of Shoreditch was founded in 1900-1. Pitfield Street, north of Old Street, and at the heart of the now fashionable Shoreditch, was chosen as the site for a new technical institute, museum, library, public baths and the gorgeously-named 'Combined Electricity and Dust Destruction Undertaking'. The public baths, built in 1899, had a special relationship with the Dust Destructor, which generated electricity and steam by burning rubbish. This meant that the Pitfield Street Baths and Washhouses dispensed with the need for boilers; instead it had condensers, which were fed by the exhaust steam from the neighbouring generating station, providing heat for the pools. The laundry was, in addition, heated from the same source, while the machinery was also driven from the power that was generated next door. The Dust

Destructing electricity generator apparently saved the Baths a lot of money on electricity bills and presumably helped keep the streets clean too.

Public baths and washhouses, or laundries, were an essential part of public services designed to improve public health and hygiene. One of the reasons the Victorians built so many of them was that they were often the sole means whole swathes of the population had of washing their clothes and washing themselves properly. A local councillor is recorded as having remarked in 1904 that there was scarcely one house in the whole of Haggerston that had a bath. Whether he was exaggerating or not, the statement gives a sense of the perceived problem of uncleanliness and the consequent disease that lurked in cities at the time. Perhaps more surprisingly, in 1930 permission was granted to increase the number of women's slipper baths at Pitfield Street. Slipper baths, as the name suggests, were slipper-shaped

Far left: The Public Baths and Washhouses – a climatic end to the ensemble of public buildings, c.1900.

Above: The Library (extant) and Public Baths, c.1899

bathtubs, usually set out in long partitioned rows within public baths. In this case, the women only had 15 slipper baths whereas the men had 56. Long queues of women would build up in Shoreditch, with waiting times of at least an hour.

By all accounts, the swimming baths and washing facilities were sumptuously appointed. Lengthy descriptions in the local newspapers of the time relate in great detail what materials were used in the building and how every aspect was innovative and cleverly designed. Each slipper bath was made from porcelain, with partitions of marble or slate, and all wooden fittings were made from teak. The same standards of construction applied to the swimming pools, lined with 'first class ivory-white tiles'. It is important to remember that the pool halls were community spaces, and used for other activities for half the year (controversially, from 1911 the Metropolitan Borough of Shoreditch gave permission for Pitfield Street Baths to be used for boys' boxing classes). Much was made of the spectators' facilities in the first-class men's pool, with its three large balconies. The changing rooms that lined the outside of the pool could also ingeniously fold away against the walls to make more space.

The Shoreditch Vestry had decided that the Public Baths and Municipal Library should be one large project and housed in one building. H A Hare had won the competition to design the Baths and Library in 1895, as his composition for the exterior was considered by far and away the most successful. However, his plan for the organisation of the interior was not the best of the entries, so it was decided that the proficient public baths architects Henry Spalding and Alfred W S Cross should be joint architects with Hare.

Spalding and Cross had been responsible for the public baths on East Dulwich Road in South London, which had proved their remarkable skill

for making the best use of awkward sites. The building's external elevations would have been comparable in design with St Pancras Public Baths and Washhouses by T W Aldwinckle (now Kentish Town Baths and recently restored), which were constructed around the same time as those on Pitfield Street. They were both built in an asymmetric Flemish style, with Renaissance details and Art Nouveau lettering that indicated the building's function and entrances. The whole elevation was constructed from red brick with stone bands and dressings. The striped turret at the north end of the library, with its steeply pitched roof surmounted by a chimney, still makes an arresting sight and would have been balanced by the three gables, now reduced to two, along the Pitfield Street elevation. The highly decorative baths elevation would have provided a climactic end to the ensemble.

In 1941, during the Second World War, the Baths suffered some minor damage, and in 1942 the state of the library's roof, situated next door, was sufficiently dangerous to require partial demolition. Although funding was secured from the War Damage Committee for the Baths to be repaired, they were closed again by the early 1960s. The soon to-be-replaced Metropolitan Borough of Shoreditch was keen for new facilities, and leased the site to National Car Parks in 1962 on condition that they demolish the Baths. The site is now replaced by a building that very consciously echoes the style and materials of the entrance to the Baths.

Pitfield Street Baths and Washhouses had retained their popularity when they reopened after the war in 1951, still performing a public service both for entertainment and hygiene. Victorian public baths were special buildings, and their value has so often been recognised all too late in our sometimes blind pursuit of progress.

Far left: The highly decorative 'male' and 'female' entrances to the baths with 'Shoreditch Public Baths' in Art Nouveau lettering above.

Above: The striped turret of the former library at the north end of the complex, 2008.

Chris Dorley-Brown

Trowbridge Estate

Deverill, Aldbourne, Wishford, Northaird, Hilmarton, Highworth and Hannington Points

Hackney Wick E9

Architects Bureau d'Etudes Techniques, Harris and Sutherland Chartered Civil Engineers of London and Centerprise Building Systems Ltd 1967-70 | demolished 1985-93

The mixture of explosive was just right, 80% Gelimex and 20% Gurit A, the latter a favourite of rock blasters. They weren't taking any chances this time. Highworth Point exploded with such intensity, that, standing a 100 yards away, you could feel the shock-wave collide with your stomach. Photographs taken at the time (12 noon sharp on 7th September 1986) show seven huge jets of smoke and debris appearing on the southern side of the 21-storey block, one every three floors. It looked like a vertical battleship firing all its cannon in a painting of an ancient sea battle. A delay of two seconds and the pre-weakened structure imploded on itself in a shroud of white and yellow dust.

This was Hackney's second 'blowdown'. The first, ten months earlier, had been a public relations disaster. Northaird Point had not completely fallen, despite its lower half having been vaporised. It was left as an embarrassing, angled stump of 12 storeys. 'The leaning tower of 'Ackney', was how the

broadcaster Derek Jameson wittily described the scene as he commentated live for BBC Radio London. It was 17 years since Ronan Point, once visible to residents of Hackney Wick across the marshes, had partially succumbed to the explosive power of British Gas just two months after completion. It appeared the game was up for Hackney's high-rises.

The Trowbridge Road project was built in two phases. The first phase was approved in 1964 and consisted of four 21-storey towers (Aldbourne, Deverill, Hannington and Hilmarton Points). The second phase, known as the Trowbridge Road extension, was approved in 1966 and consisted of three further 21-storey towers (Highworth, Northaird and Wishford Points). Construction was complete by 1970.

For the Trowbridge Estate project the Greater London Council (GLC) had obtained an off-the-

Far left: The demolition of Northaird Point on 3 November 1985.

Above: The leaning tower of 'Ackney, 1985.

shelf design from French architects Bureau d'Etudes Techniques for a quick-and-easy build that had worked very successfully as naval quarters in *Mers-el-Kebir* in Algeria, on the Gulf of Oran where the annual rainfall equals that of about three weeks in Hackney. The nature of the design meant that the majority of the load was carried on the outside walls and this proved to be the building's problem. The large slab concrete design had acted like blotting paper in the 15 years the blocks had been standing, the concrete panels that formed the outside walls were not weather-resistant. They let in both wind and rain, making the apartments cold and damp, prime breeding ground for cockroaches.

Two months after Northaird Point refused to come tumbling down Brian Sedgemore, the local Member of Parliament, told the House of Commons:

"The Trowbridge Estate was built amid the naiveté and optimism of the 1960s. Today it embodies the pessimism of the 1980s. It is a monument to misery and insensitivity, which demonstrates only too clearly how that which can be fashionable but which is not rooted in the needs of the people can quickly become a disaster.

The high-rise fiasco that has caused so much pain and hurt to 542 families on the Trowbridge Estate began in something of the atmosphere of the South Sea Bubble. The developers, J M Hill, rubbed their hands with glee at the thought of quick-and-easy profits. The architects believed that they would be remembered for pinpointing a part of London's skyline. The politicians thought that they would receive the plaudits of the crowd for getting things done. The civil servants

Above right: The remaining towers of the Trowbridge Estate, 1987.

Above: BBC Radio cab with 30-foot aerial, 1985.

congratulated themselves on master-minding what was supposed to be a munificent operation.

What can be said about the flats and the estate today? First, they are slums. Water penetrates from the outside and condensation corrodes the steel from the inside. Secondly, the developers, architects, politicians and civil servants would not have dreamt of living in the brutal, hideous, inconsequential, soul-destroying and criminal folly that today we call Trowbridge. Thirdly, the people were never consulted about whether what was being built suited their needs and those of their children."

Hackney once boasted 122 tower blocks (I am using my own criteria here, a tower block being a residential building over nine storeys). The Nightingale, Holly Street, New Kingshold, Kings Crescent and Clapton Park estates were all levelled (bar three token refurbished and recladded blocks) and, in all, 23 of these huge monoliths disappeared between 1985 and 2002.

But these beasts are not giving in easily. Nearly 100 blocks still remain today and in most cases they are in good condition: concierges and CCTV have been installed, draughty entrance halls sealed, roofs sympathetically pitched to divert the rain, PVC window frames replacing aluminium and wood. In some cases the clean modern lines have been appended with studs, louvres and disguising paint jobs as in Lincoln Court. Balconies have been sealed as in Welshpool House. By and large though, the dramatic social experiment remains fairly intact and is now inspiring a new generation of tower blocks that are beginning to pierce the borough's skyline, but none has yet approached the misguided bravura of those pioneer post-war buildings.

Ray Rogers

Woodberry Down Comprehensive School

Woodberry Down N4

Architect London County Council 1955 | demolished 1999

The Woodberry Down Comprehensive School was important for several reasons: it was the first planned comprehensive school in London; its architecture reflected a continental Modernism that influenced school design nationally; it had several works of art from the 1951 Festival of Britain; it was the centrepiece of the socially progressive Woodberry Down Estate; and it was a highly successful school that helped to popularise comprehensive education.

The school, which opened in 1955, was a product of the LCC Architects' Department. Much of the design has been attributed to Joseph Berger, a Czech-born pupil of Adolph Loos, who came to Britain in 1936 from Palestine where he had set up practice in 1934. He worked on the *County of London Plan* with Forshaw and Abercrombie before joining the LCC schools division in 1945. Design work on the school started in 1947 and the final layout was established by 1949.

Construction started in October 1950, but steel shortages meant that work on the concrete superstructure was delayed until November 1952. The completed school showed a strong continental influence in its design. The main impact externally came from the scale and massing of the blocks and the bold use of contrasting cladding within the highly ordered grid of the concrete frame that resulted in a simple and striking group of buildings.

Information about the school was widely published on its completion, with much interest shown in the prefabricated concrete structure for which Felix Samuely was the engineer. Samuely worked on a number of well-known and innovative buildings, including Erich Mendelsohn's De La Warr Pavilion in Bexhill-on-Sea. The columns and staircases were cast *in situ,* but the rest of the frame was composed of precast concrete edge and spine beams, precast pre-stressed main beams and precast floor slabs.

Above: Headmistress's office, c.1955.

The exposed concrete frame was painted and the wall surfaces infilled with either purple or yellow stock brick or precast concrete panels faced with white spar (stone chippings) or crushed gravel. The building's metal windows gave the blocks a strong horizontal emphasis, and the whole feeling was of well-ordered modern spaces filled with light.

The Modernist credo was also expressed in the layout of the school, designed to bring sunlight and fresh air to all rooms, with the spaces between the buildings designed for play and recreation. The buildings were arranged around two courtyards. Those grouped around the smaller courtyard were two storeys high containing the main entrance, offices, and assembly and dining halls. Extending west were three four-storey teaching blocks forming a large U-shape, with two detached gymnasia further to the west. The main classroom block had a spectacular view south over the reservoir. The north block, the only one surviving, is notable for the single-storey workshop at street level with its folded slab roof and north light formed by an *in situ* concrete vierendeel girder with hexagonal glazed openings. The two detached gymnasia were also bold structures, each having a thin concrete 'W' section folded shell roof that spanned sixty feet between two pairs of columns.

The architecturally most striking feature was the assembly hall with its hexagonal folded shell roof, designed to accommodate the whole school population of 1,250 in one sitting. The roof was formed of a latticed steel skin structure spanning a hexagonal area of 83 feet by 75 feet and 8 feet in depth. The large cantilevered gallery was supported at only three points, the construction forming a torque beam of great stiffness, allowing the area below the gallery to be kept free of columns. With its timber panelling and a sense of enclosure achieved by the large gallery and unusual shape, the hall was described by Miss

Chetwyn, the school's first headteacher, as "having something of grandeur".

The school had an art department, and staff and pupils created two large murals depicting construction sites on the Woodberry Down Estate. It would be nice to think they drew inspiration from the school's three notable works of art, two of them relocated from the Festival of Britain's South Bank exhibition, including a large oil painting by Carel Weight, a relief panel of Viking ships by Anthony Gilbert (carved by H J Eric Smith) and a sculpture by C W Lewis set in an ornamental pool in the small courtyard.

The story of Woodberry Down Comprehensive School, its birth and initial success then decline and demolition, mirrors a much wider betrayal of the LCC's post-war idealism that had created a new community at Woodberry Down. Structural faults (perhaps partly due to the post-war steel shortage) had plagued the estate and some of the housing blocks had been declared unsafe by the late 1980s. In 1996 the school's main classroom block was suffering badly from settlement. However, the school's decline had set in much earlier. The rise in school leaving age had seen the school population reach 1,300 by the early 1970s but a later fall in numbers led to its amalgamation with the larger Clissold Park School in 1982. The Woodberry Down site was adapted as a Further Education Centre but this was finally closed in 1995. The school was belatedly considered for listing in 1999 but by then it was too late and the die was cast. The surviving technical block and one of the two gymnasia are all that now remain and are in use as the Beis Chinuch Lebonos Jewish Girls' School. Unlike the contemporary Woodberry Down Primary School and John Scott Health Centre, both of which are now listed Grade II, the rest of the school buildings were demolished and the site left abandoned and awaiting redevelopment.

Far left: Corridor in Science Block, 1955.

Above left: In the foreground the single-storey woodwork block with hexagonal north lights, c.1955.

Above: Internal courtyard, 1955.

Ignored

in need of some love and attention

"To remove buildings from the ['Buildings at Risk'] register requires a combination of persuasion, incentive and statutory action, but above all support..."

English Heritage, 'Heritage at Risk', 2009

Left: Projected glazed lift and stair tower, Space Studios, 2009.

Interior,

David Solman

Abney Park Chapel

Abney Park Cemetery N16

Architect William Hosking 1840-1 | listed Grade II | on 'Buildings at Risk' register (condition – very bad)

If you are beginning to think about architecture and its relationship to landscape, or looking for an architectural expression of religious harmony, you might take a closer look at the non-denominational Abney Park Chapel.

Dating from 1840-1, the chapel and its 32-acre setting formed one of the 'magnificent seven' cemeteries established in a ring around London, while also serving educational and botanical functions. Its centrepiece – the Abney Park Chapel – was open to all. The foundation stone was laid on 20 May 1840 by Sir Chapman Marshall, Lord Mayor of the City of London. Parties were free to choose their own chaplains, but the Reverend J Kershaw for the Church of England, and Reverend John Jefferson for Congregationalists, would otherwise officiate.

An ecumenical building of a similar type, though in classical style, had been attempted previously.

A non-denominational cemetery chapel had been built in the 1820s for the more compact five-acre necropolis in the north of England at Low Hill, Everton. But nothing similar had been attempted in the vicinity of London, and there was nothing on this scale.

The cultural, landscape and architectural significance of this building has been recognised in modern times. It was listed in 1975, when the Chapel's fortunes and those of its woodland burial gardens were at their lowest ebb. The special scenic quality of the chapel was specifically recognised in its listing statement; and was given further recognition when the whole park was listed as a Historic Park and Garden in 1987.

From the outset, these scenic qualities of the park and Chapel struck a chord. Writing in 1843, the architectural, landscape and horticultural critic John Claudius Loudon praised Abney Park as "the

Far left: The derelict chapel, 2009.

Above: Interior, 2009.

most ornamental cemetery in the neighbourhood of London." If one agrees that here the founding trustees had succeeded in creating a picturesque pattern of buildings and landscaped spaces, its centrepiece was surely the imaginative Chapel?

Exacting standards had certainly been demonstrated in the Chapel's composition and construction. The master craftsman and builder John Jay, whose Victoria Tower at the Houses of Parliament is internationally renowned, was chosen both for the hand-carved stonework and general construction. The role of architect was given to William Hosking FSA who, shortly after completing this chapel and another in Poplar, was appointed Professor of Architecture at King's College London; while the Chapel's landscape setting was entrusted to George Loddiges of Hackney's most prestigious nursery firm.

As with all good design, the team was completed with active client involvement. In this capacity, George Collison's immense influence can be seen in guiding the various iterations of chapel design, as well as legal aspects of managing such projects.

Built in warm, yellow stock bricks with stone dressings, redolent of a north European brick Gothic style, with a polychromatic steeple rising to 120 feet, the Chapel stood out as a landmark from the northern heights of Woodberry Down and surpassed the height of St Mary's Church in Stoke Newington. The south-facing façade was highly ornamental. Framed by a pair of octagonal turrets, it all but enticed the public to ascend newel staircases to a galleried first floor below an imposing ten-part rose window. A carved ogee arch in Bath stone completed the effect. Elsewhere, stained glass donated by Dr Nathaniel Rogers added colour; and mullioned windows – romanticised in Gothic novels – captured the light of the sun through east- and west-facing rose windows above.

As to its general style, the Chapel, though following Gothic Revival principles, also showed originality. Conceived early in the Gothic Revival period – in the first years of the Victorian era, well before the drama of High Victorian Gothic – such

Above: Interior, 2009.

originality was somewhat controversial. No doubt this rather suited an architect and scholar such as William Hosking, a man later likened by *The Builder* to Lord Brougham, and who in later life dared to publish suspicions of plagiarism against the British Museum.

Whereas some Gothic Revival architects refused commissions for unconsecrated or non-conformist chapels, Hosking rose above his factionalised peers. Commencing with a conventional High Church design, he prepared iterations to suit his independent-minded clients and their budget – a style later termed Dissenting Gothic. Of course, for the traditionalist, there were elements they could enjoy. The chapel incorporated rose windows copied from Beverley Minster, and a broach spire – recognisably 14th-century Decorated Gothic in style – copied from Bloxham Church in Oxfordshire.

The whole effect provided just the right blend of dissenting simplicity and High Church ornamentation. Its design and materials conveyed the quiet demeanour of London's only non-conformist-owned garden cemetery, while featuring an almost theatrical backdrop to the Chapel's approach by foot from the village of Stoke Newington on Church Street – Dr Watts' Walk.

Today this scenic Gothic chapel in the heart of the woods of Abney Park is believed to be the oldest surviving non-denominational chapel in Europe, and William Hosking's only surviving public building. Much photographed and admired, it is in demand as the backdrop to occasional drama productions, children's events, and other cultural attractions. Yet it stands neglected and disused.

The present owners, Hackney Council and the Abney Park Trust, have re-roofed and underpinned the chapel, which has helped keep it standing since its owning company became insolvent in the 1970s and left it all but abandoned. However, it still awaits its Prince Charming to bring it alive for modern-day educational, cultural and heritage audiences.

Let's hope this fine building, one of Hackney's most important historic treasures, currently on English Heritage's 'Building at Risk' register, is restored and reopened soon.

2013 update:
The chapel is still on English Heritage's Buildings at Risk register, with Abney Park Trust currently in negotiations with Hackney Council concerning the future of the cemetery and park. Contact: abneyparkcemetery@gmail.com

Sarah Wise

Cleeve Workshops

Calvert Avenue E2

Architect Reginald Minton-Taylor 1895-8 | listed Grade II | on 'Buildings at Risk' register (condition – poor)

George Herbert Little felt cheated when, in the autumn of 1896, he found himself among the first to rent one of the London County Council's Cleeve Workshops. In a peevish ten-page letter, written on 21 October, Mr Little berated the Council for having tempted him on to the brand-new Boundary Street Estate with the promise of a purpose-built workshop (just across the yard from his flat in Cleeve House); what, in fact, the LCC had erected were "sheds, not workshops", he wrote. He was not one ever to listen to the opinions of the fair sex, he continued; nevertheless, he had to agree with his good lady wife when she stated her belief that the poor maintenance of the Estate, and the absence of a qualified caretaker, were already resulting in shabbiness at Cleeve.

Fast-forward 113 years, and the workshops are only now starting to emerge from decades of neglect. Always a poor relation of the two other surviving

Boundary Street Estate sets of workshops – behind Marlow House and Sunbury House – Cleeve had for many years looked very sorry for itself. However, Cleeve Workshops' latest owner – a Clerkenwell-based estate agent – has been hard at work in 2009 refurbishing them, in the hope of attracting the type of tenants (artists, craftspeople, film production teams and other media firms) who rent at Sunbury and Marlow.

There's a lack of magnificence at Cleeve: where Sunbury and Marlow are two storeys, Cleeve Workshops are comparatively stunted. But their large front windows, skylighting and 200-foot floor space mean they could scrub up well to carry on the tradition of artisan work on the Boundary Street Estate.

Their recent, beaten-up appearance belies their historical significance. Cleeve Workshops are a physical manifestation of a change in the way of

Above: The once sad and dilapidated Cleeve Workshops, 2008.

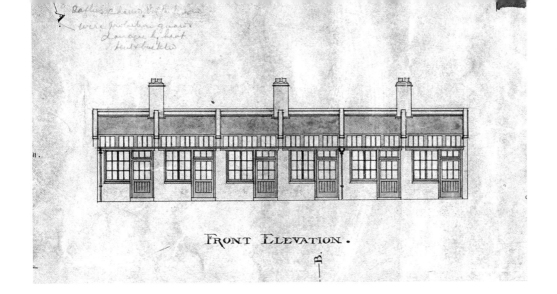

FRONT ELEVATION.

thinking about working-class housing at the turn of the 20th century. In Shoreditch in general, and in this small corner in particular, the furniture trade was the dominant industry in the second half of the 19th century. Woodworking employed one-fifth of the adult residents of the Old Nichol slum, upon which the Boundary Street Estate was built between 1894 and 1900. Ernest Aves, one of Charles Booth's researchers for *The Life and Labour of the People in London* survey, wrote that: "From the East End workshops…produce goes out of every description, from the richly inlaid cabinet that may be sold for £100, or the carved chair that can be made to pass as rare 'antique' workmanship, down to the gypsy tables that the maker sells for 9s a dozen, or the cheap bedroom suites and duchesse tables that are now flooding the market." It was an intensely competitive trade, with mass, 'slop' work being produced on spec, in the hope of a quick sale to one of the wholesalers of Curtain Road and Charlotte Road.

Boundary Street Estate was London's first large-scale council estate and one of the nation's most important experiments in municipal housing. It embodied the notion of integrated living pursued by the Progressive Party, who ran the LCC for 18 years from its inception in 1889. These Romantic-Socialist idealists wanted artisan workers to be able to rent clean, large, comfortable work-spaces just yards from their new council homes. This was the LCC's response to the conditions found within the Nichol, where most of the self-employed small manufacturers had had to keep the machinery, tools and noxious substances of their trades within their tiny and dilapidated residential spaces. For some, though, old habits died hard. One E C Barratt was evicted within weeks of moving into the Cleeve buildings: an LCC snooper had discovered that Barratt, a tailor, was employing two girls to work alongside him within his small flat – effectively running a tiny 'manufactory' in what had been designated purely domestic premises. Barratt was urged to take up the offer of

a workshop, but declined and had his tenancy terminated.

The Boundary Street Estate was the creation of the brilliant young team in the LCC's Architects' Department. Among the most sublime blocks were those of the relatively obscure Reginald Minton-Taylor, designer of the Cleeve Workshops. Minton-Taylor was the great-grandson of the Minton Potteries' founder; and between 1884 and 1887 he worked in the office of Peter Paul Pugin, and made a special study of brick architecture in Holland and eastern England. Later, he would express wry contempt for many East Enders' disdain for the 'Cahnty Cahncil's' (his mocking phrase) experiments at Boundary Street.

Four sets of workshops were constructed at Boundary Street, but those on Swanfield Street were demolished in the early 1970s, shortly before the Boundary Street Estate was listed. In 1985, the Estate was designated a conservation area by the London Borough of Tower Hamlets. Cleeve's potential problem is that in a bizarre borough boundary dog-leg, it is within Hackney, not Tower Hamlets, and therefore falls outside the Boundary Estate Conservation Area. However, good news came in early February 2009, when Hackney decided to include the dog-leg within the South Shoreditch Conservation Area. Though this, along with being listed Grade II, does offer protection, the City Fringe is a perilous place for a building to be sited. A report submitted to Hackney Council in January 2009 has written of "the 'wall' of…office developments [that] appears almost like a giant wave about to break over the southern half of South Shoreditch." Local residents (and those non-residents who also cherish the Estate) worry that the Cleeve Workshops are vulnerable, especially when the bust ends and the next boom begins. The Workshops are integral to the 'working village' vision dreamt up on the LCC's drawing boards in the 1890s. It would be sad if Cleeve's littleness, and the obscurity of their creator, should ever lead to their demise.

2013 update:
Some workshops have been refurbished and in use, others still require repair.

Far left: Cleeve Workshops, c.1950s.

Above left: London County Council's workshop, 1895.

Above: The single-storey Cleeve workshops on the left overshadowed by the Cleeve block (right) on the Boundary Street Estate, c.1900.

John O'Callaghan and the Haggerston Pool Community Trust

Haggerston Baths

Whiston Road E2

Architect A W S Cross 1904 | listed Grade II | on 'Buildings at Risk' register (condition – poor)

Haggerston Baths were opened on 25th June 1904 by the Mayor of Shoreditch. At the opening swimming gala, the Vice-Chair of the Baths and Washhouses Committee, Mr B J Wakeling, was cheered by watching crowds as he swam the length of the pool under water.

Wakeling, also the secretary of a large London swimming club, was unhappy about the lack of pools being provided under the 1878 legislation (which allowed local authorities to borrow money to build indoor swimming pools). He described the primary object of his role in local government to be about "public baths in Shoreditch or elsewhere". He also thought "great care should be taken, that no inducements are offered to cause the public washhouse to become popular with any members of the community other than the poorest".

The architect Alfred Cross (1858-1932), shared Wakeling's passion for public health and

cleanliness. In partnership with his son, K M B Cross, he had become England's leading design specialist for public baths – responsible for the design of Pitfield Street Baths, Ironmonger Row, Camberwell, Dulwich and Marshall Street Baths, to name but a few.

Haggerston Baths are built in the Edwardian Baroque style. The building is constructed of soft red brick in English bond with Portland stone dressings, and is topped with a cupola with Ionic columns, leaded dome and gilded weathervane in the form of a ship. This 'Golden Hind' (which has become the Baths unofficial symbol) was made by the Salford firm George Wragge Ltd. The slate roof, also, resembles the upturned hull of a ship and it has been rumoured that the industrial-scale boilers to heat the water for the pool and baths were salvaged from a ship. Originally, there was a 100 feet by 35 feet swimming pool with 11 first-class and 30 second-class slipper baths, and a washhouse.

Far left: The impressive south elevation with entrances for 'men' and 'women', 2008.

Above: Interior, 2009.

Swimming pools built under the 1878 Act were to open for five summer months only (until filtration arrived in the 1920s). So in winter the pool was emptied and a floor was laid transforming the space into a hall.

The washhouse, approached from the back of the building, was built without architectural pretension; but inside were to be found the most up-to-date washing troughs, wringing and mangling machines, and a large drying chamber.

Janet Entwistle, as a child, lived in the flat at the top of the building when her father was the Superintendent of Haggerston and Pitfield Street Baths from 1949-55. When the family moved there the pool was still closed, following bomb damage during the Second World War. She remembers pigeons nesting in the big shrapnel holes at the front of the building, but adds "all the time we were at Haggerston new improvements were being made". Alongside the hustle and bustle of the laundry and baths, she describes a café and club-room with darts and snooker and the 'pink parlour' downstairs rented out for wedding parties and events. There were also water polo sessions run by the local banks. She recalls "Midland [came] on a Monday, Cornhill on a Wednesday and Lloyds on a Thursday." Entwistle also remembers the coal-fired Lancashire boilers that heated the laundry and baths:

"The men below stairs were always called by their formal names, they were generally men of few words and much coal dust, but nevertheless very kind. I would go into the noisy black place where two magnificent furnaces were fed with coal, which arrived in huge piles, tipped off the back of a lorry. I was allowed to shovel the coal into a neater pile as it got scattered during the shovelling. When the furnace doors were opened, the fires glowed from orange to white and the heat was tremendous."

Considerable alterations were made to the baths in the 1960s, and then in the 1980s a new boiler was installed, and the pool itself was reduced to a 25-metre pool (from 30.5 metres), with a teaching pool at the back end. New changing rooms were built and all the old changing cubicles and poolside seating was taken out and a balcony added, making more room for swimmers and coaches, and for officials during competitions.

Despite alterations, the Baths were listed in 1988 due partly to the impressive south façade and first floor loggia with paired columns with Ionic capitals. The baths also have an innovative internal roof structure to create a pool hall with less echo and more natural light. They would have been a grand addition to an area consisting of ordinary terraced houses. English Heritage reported that "The Baths are a unique and important part of Hackney's heritage."

From the 1980s Hackney Council allowed the building to deteriorate until suddenly on 11 February 2000 the baths were closed on safety grounds. By this point, despite being run down, Haggerston had become the central swimming pool in Hackney, with ten local primary schools using it for weekly swimming. The active and successful Haggerston Swimming Club, run by Wally Tassell from 1964-90, was one of eight sports clubs using the pool at the time.

Following closure, a campaign started in the local community calling for the re-opening of the pool. This prompted the establishment of Haggerston Pool Community Trust, which initially organised meetings, protests, petitions and candlelit vigils.

From 2004 the Trust started to organise the annual Laburnum Street Party, attracting thousands of local people and featuring a children's parade demanding the re-opening of the pool. The public's affection for the building has been shown by the large numbers taking advantage of the occasional tours, including Open House 2003 when over 700 people eagerly came to visit the pool, with many travelling long distances to revive childhood memories.

As Hackney Council's financial situation improved, they started to respond more favourably to local demands. A detailed feasibility study was published in 2006 and proposals to redevelop the pool into a Health and Wellbeing Centre were endorsed by the Council's Cabinet in March 2009. Currently a team is being appointed to develop a plan and source the funds. The building remains a reminder of the high municipal ideals of the then Metropolitan Borough of Shoreditch. In the words of Ian Gordon and Simon Inglis, authors of *Great Lengths: the Historic Indoor Swimming Pools of Britain* "we can only hope that someone senior at Hackney Council is practising their underwater swimming, ready for the big day at Haggerston".

This contribution is based on an article written by the late John O'Callaghan in 2003.

Above: The cupola with Ionic columns and 'golden hind' weathervane.

2013 update:
The Haggerston Pool Campaign is still fighting for the baths to be reopened. See www.haggerstonpool.org.uk

Isobel Watson

New Lansdowne Club

Mare Street E8

Architect unknown *c.*1699 | listed Grade II* | on 'Buildings at Risk' register (condition – poor)

Since Sutton House's future was secured, 195 Mare Street – best known in its most recent incarnation as the New Lansdowne Club – has been Hackney's saddest story. It is the only survivor from the range of substantial villas (of both earlier and later date) which was until the later 19th century the defining feature of once-opulent Mare Street. This makes its current state all the more tragic.

The house stands towards the front of what began as an awkward, T-shaped site, and may have been infill on the ground of a nearby building. It is in brown brick with red dressings, detached, with three floors over a basement and five bays to front and rear. The top floor has sloping roofs behind a parapet, which led to an assumption that the structure dates to the 18th century, before 1716 when the earliest parish records show it occupied by Daniel Dolins. However, a feasibility study conducted by Rees Bolter Architects in 1997 for

Hackney Council and English Heritage identified that the parapet post-dates the structure, and that the original roofline had been raised. As built, the roof appears to have been pitched, at a steeper angle, with overhanging eaves, a formation characteristic of the later 17th century. The discovery of correspondence which indicates a date between autumn 1697 and summer 1699 for the Dolins family's move to Hackney is therefore consistent with the builder's commissioning client being Abraham Dolins the younger (d.1706), a successful merchant whose father had settled in London from Ghent in the early 1600s. Even if he purchased a pre-existing structure, however, Abraham enlarged and altered the accommodation in 1700, on his son Daniel's marriage, for the requirements of the couple and their eventual offspring.

The history of the house has four phases. For the first 150 years it served as a family home, with

Above: The forlorn New Lansdowne Club, 2009.

stabling and about an acre of garden: a classic suburban villa for City people. It was owned and used successively by two families. Dolins' heirs held it throughout the 18th century. Daniel Dolins trained in theology and law, was knighted in 1722 and figured among the great and the good of his time; in Hackney parish he was the leading local citizen after the lord of the manor. After the death of the last Dolins, the house was sold in 1801 to a relative of Thomas Wilson, another City merchant, who married a Hackney woman of Swiss descent. He served in Parliament as a Tory, representing City financial interests, in the 1820s. His opposition to the electoral reform bill of 1832 led to a narrow escape, when the bill became law, from having his windows smashed during local celebrations.

In 1860 the house entered the second phase of its history when it passed from Wilson's daughter to the trustees of a charity founded to commemorate the prison reformer Elizabeth Fry (d.1845). The project grew out of Fry's involvement with the British Ladies' Society for Promoting the Reformation of Female Prisoners, and typifies the making-over of merchants' villas for institutional uses in this period. The first Elizabeth Fry Refuge was established in 1849 in leasehold premises at Cambridge Heath Road, to provide residence in a secure and secluded environment, and training for domestic service, for young women who had completed prison sentences, mostly for very minor offences. It moved to No. 195 Mare Street when the freehold was acquired, for £2,100, in March 1860.

On acquisition the house contained 11 bedrooms on the two upper floors; large drawing and dining rooms, the servants' hall and a water closet on the ground floor; and kitchens and cellars in the basement. The alterations mainly affected the latter, resulting in a communal dining room for the young women; and additional water closets

which were provided in an outbuilding. Pedestrian access by way of a path opposite the front door replaced the carriage sweep and older gates.

The residents, usually about 20 in number, stayed between a few weeks and 12 months, up to a hundred passing through the house in a typical year. They were put to laundry and needlework, as training and to supplement funds. The managers – initially a committee of ladies for domestic and pastoral issues, and a committee of gentlemen for the finances – devised incentives to encourage former residents to demonstrate behaviour that was "respectable, neat, and quiet", religious observance and temperance being much encouraged.

The back part of the garden was sold in 1875 to local builders, for Gransden and Fortescue Avenues. The constant need for repairs, especially to the walls, became a year-on-year drain on resources; a move was decided in 1911 when "the walls threatened to collapse". In 1913 the Refuge moved to Highbury, and the property was sold to a local social club with liberal/radical roots with which it has been associated ever since. In this third phase of its history the house underwent its most radical structural changes. A concert hall was constructed at the rear, outbuildings were replaced and a billiard room created on the first floor. Some rebuilding of the front wall and top floor followed bomb damage in 1940.

Social and demographic change forced the decline of the working men's club, and brought in the fourth phase: dereliction, squatting and casual vandalism. Schemes for redevelopment have been debated and one, using the core building for a community centre, has been approved. Implementation of a rescue plan – phase five – is keenly awaited.

2013 update:
The house has now been sold.

Far left: Exterior, 1942.

Above: Ground floor room with original fireplace missing. Over the last two months looters have stolen many original features, including fireplaces and metalwork, 2009.

Suzanne Waters

Nicholl House (and Needwood House)

Woodberry Down Estate N4

Architect London County Council 1946-9 | threatened with demolition

With its identical twin Needwood House, Nicholl House, is one of the four eight-storey blocks on the Woodberry Down Estate. The estate was one of the largest and most ambitious, built by the London County Council (LCC) in the 1940s. These two blocks, with their deep overhanging eaves, bold profiles and cantilevered balconies on the upper floors, appear redolent of a continental Modernism and represent a sharp departure from inter-war schemes. Now, with the complete redevelopment of the estate, they face an uncertain future.

What is curious is no one knows for sure who designed them. The most likely candidate is John Henry Forshaw, the architect to the LCC from 1941-5. Responsible for the layout of the whole estate, he had advocated the building of these more expensive eight-storey blocks. This had been in part prompted by the 1943 *County of London Plan*, which he had co-authored with town planner Sir Patrick Abercrombie. One of the most influential documents on post-war planning, it advocated a radical rethink on housing provision from what had gone hitherto. Instead of slum-clearance programmes and the building of vast cottage estates on the outer fringes, London was to be divided into a series of 'zones', in which a higher density of housing would be allocated to the central area and a lower density to the outer boroughs. One of its principal recommendations was to accommodate different sizes of family. The new housing would follow the continental model (as seen in Sweden) of a mixture of high-rise and low-rise apartment blocks and houses.

Woodberry Down had been planned before the war, when the LCC had an active policy of slum clearance, which included moving people out of the congested inner city areas to the suburbs and, in the late 1930s, this part of Stoke Newington was deemed suburbia. An estate was planned on a site

Far left: The stark west elevation of Nicholl House, c.1948.

Above: After years of neglect Nicholl House is now in desperate need of refurbishment, 2009.

overlooking the reservoirs near to the New River in 1936. The initial scheme in 1938 comprised a number of two-to five-storey blocks arranged in a massive horseshoe. But in 1943, as the *County of London Plan* was coming to fruition, a new scheme was put forward, which was in essence the one built. This was a layout whereby most of the blocks were laid out in parallel lines orientated north-south at right angles to the reservoirs but on a diagonal with Lordship Road. Forshaw's introduction of the eight-storey blocks was to avoid the monotony of rows of 'walk-up' blocks of five storeys, with long balconies and hipped roofs. There were also three-storey blocks with maisonettes and two-storey blocks of flats for older people. The scheme was approved in 1943, albeit with reservations about costs by the LCC's Valuer, Cyril Walker. Until the end of war, there was a running battle between Forshaw, who wanted high standards, and the Valuer, who was concerned with costs and fast production. Forshaw resigned in 1945 and the whole allocation of post-war housing design and production was transferred to the Valuer's Department. Fortunately, the final layout, including the eight-storey blocks, was approved a month before Forshaw's resignation, so he can be claimed as the designer.[1]

The eight-storey blocks were built of concrete, as steel and brick were in short supply after the war. The façades faced east–west, so that all rooms received sunshine throughout the day, but were placed far enough apart to allow for plenty of light and air. Accommodation was generous, each block providing 79 flats, ranging from one to four bedrooms (with built-in cupboards) and a separate bathroom and WC. Five lifts as well as staircases were provided, which opened on to balconies to the three upper floors. In 1949, the first blocks to be completed were Nicholl House and Needwood House. They were centrally heated, albeit with just one radiator in the largest bedroom and the living room, plus an electric fire. Originally, the exteriors were painted in cream and light blue called 'Tyrolean roughcast'.

Above right: Nicholl House just after completion, c.1949.

Above: Sign for Nicholl House, 2009.

There has been speculation as to the inspiration for their striking design. No doubt, some ideas came from Europe before the war, as continental Modernism impacted on British architecture.[2] During the war, neutral countries like Sweden continued to design modern public housing. In September 1943, the *Architectural Review* devoted a whole issue to Swedish architecture, paving the way for Swedish influence on post-war British housing. But much closer to home in nearby Amhurst Road is Evelyn Court, an estate of ten five-storey 'walk-up' blocks designed by Burnet, Tait & Lorne for the Four Per Cent Industrial Dwellings Company in 1934-5. These tall, rectangular blocks, flat fronted and flat roofed (originally painted white with the central stair towers painted green), with metal windows, were not dissimilar to flats in inter-war Germany and may have inspired the design for Woodberry Down. More importantly, though, was the unique nature of their construction – a monolithic reinforced concrete frame faced in render. This system was invented by Evelyn Court's contractors Holland, Hannen & Cubitt, who subsequently used it at Woodberry Down for the eight-storey blocks.[3]

In 1947, Robert Matthew was appointed as Superintending Architect to the LCC, with Leslie Martin as his deputy. Matthew later successfully lobbied for housing to be given back to the LCC Architects' Department, following criticism of the 'Valuer's blocks' in the architectural press. As the emphasis in the 1950s swung towards point blocks and Corbusian slabs, the Woodberry Down slabs were seen as a lumpy and half-hearted Modernism.[4] Nevertheless, it is possible to appreciate their architectural and historical significance, as they represent the transition between the design of public housing by the LCC in the 1930s and the ideas for urban housing expressed by the authors of the *County of London Plan*.

2013 update:
Nicholl House is due for demolition.

Julia Lafferty and Patrick Vernon

Palace Pavilion (formerly Dougie's and Clapton Cinematograph Theatre)

Lower Clapton Road E5

Architect George Duckworth 1910 | vacant

The opening of the Clapton Cinematograph Theatre, at 229 Lower Clapton Road, was heralded for weeks beforehand by large display notices in the *Hackney and Kingsland Gazette*, proclaiming that it would be "the most luxurious and up-to-date Theatre in the district". A leading article told readers that they could expect " some of the finest pictures procurable, illustrating topical events, humorous and dramatic episodes, and scenes of travel that will introduce the audience to places and people whom they may never have a chance of seeing, except through the eye of the camera".

The cinema opened on Friday 16 December 1910 with a private function attended by the Mayor and Mayoress of Hackney, Councillor and Mrs W F Fenton-Jones.

Guests were welcomed by Mr H J Chinn, the Chairman of Clapton Cinematograph Theatre Ltd.

The *Gazette* reported that a programme of moving pictures was shown and "heartily appreciated" by the audience.

The cinema was described by the *Gazette* as an "imposing structure" of brick and concrete with a steel roof. It was designed by George Duckworth, who was also responsible for the King's Picture Palace in Kensal Rise (now demolished). Costing £4,500 to build, it must have made quite an impact. Its façade included a series of five ornamental classical pilasters with capitals. The three central pilasters were more widely spaced to accommodate two arched entrances. Cornicing and an entablature displaying 'Cinematograph Theatre' rose above, set forward from a flat-fronted dome façade, decorated with a variety of mouldings, part of which – a 'CCT' monogram – is still visible. Inside, audiences were presented with an 18 feet by 15 feet screen and raked seating, with a capacity of 850, with no balcony. This was

Above: The former Palace Pavilion 2009.

later reduced to 700 when it was renamed the Kenning Hall Cinema in 1919. Its decoration was lavish: early promotional material shows a decorated barrel-vaulted ceiling, and the *Gazette* reported that it had comfortable plush tip-up seats with a good view of the screen assured from all parts of the theatre. Advertised as "Clapton's popular family rendezvous", in its earliest days it showed one-reel silent films combined with live music performances in programmes lasting around an hour and a half.

The Clapton Cinematograph Theatre was one of a number of early cinemas, including the Electric Cinema in Portobello Road (opened in February 1910) and Duke of York's in Brighton (opened in September 1910). These and other cinemas were established following the passing of the Cinematograph Act of 1909, which required film presentations to be shown under controlled and licensed safety conditions, due to the highly inflammable nature of nitrate film when exposed to extreme heat from projector lamps. This had led to a number of instances of fires and loss of life.

The 1920s heralded the golden age of silent cinema, with screen stars such as Mary Pickford and Rudolph Valentino attracting ever larger audiences (around 20,000,000 cinema tickets were being sold weekly in Britain at this time). In 1929 the Kenning Hall was converted for sound pictures and in the late 1930s the cinema was taken over by the Odeon circuit when its frontage was modified with a simply articulated fascia in the Odeon Theatre's Modernist house style. It seems that the Odeon had a view to demolishing the building, as they bought up nearby properties with the intention of building a brand new cinema. However with the onset of the Second World War, this came to nothing, and meanwhile in October 1939 Associated British Cinemas built their much larger Deco-style, 1,884-seat Ritz Cinema at No. 217a Lower Clapton Road.

The Kenning Hall remained one of the Odeon circuit's lesser cinemas until 1958 when it was leased out to a succession of operators, including Mistlin's Theatres. In its later years the Kenning Hall became known as something of a 'flea-pit'. With declining audiences in the 1970s and with the emergence of home video, the Kenning Hall Cinema eventually closed its doors in June 1979, and lay empty and unused until it was converted into a nightclub in 1983.

The nightclub Dougie's was opened by Irvine Douglas who had previously owned a popular club and restaurant called 'Dougie's Hideaway' in Archway, London. Hackney was chosen as the location due to a growing demand, among second-and third-generation black Britons, for a venue that played black music. Having selected the site, Douglas spent considerable money converting the cinema into a venue for up to 1,200 people with a restaurant and separate lounges for women and VIPs. The building was on two levels, with a large stage for live performances.

Douglas had a clear vision. He wanted a club with high standards and a strict dress code to reflect the desires of an emerging black middle class, or Buppies (black Yuppies), in Thatcher's Britain. Douglas did not see the club as a black venue, but a place that played the best in black music from lovers rock, rare groove, rhythm and blues (R&B), soul, reggae, soca, calypso and the latest sounds from Africa. Dougie's, like other clubs at the time, created a space for home-grown music talent and a club scene very reminiscent of the house parties of the Windrush generation during the 1940s and 1950s. The club had a team of security staff, which created a safe space for clubbing with very few reported incidents of violence. The club was very popular at weekends and during holiday periods, attracting an especially large crowd for the soca night on Sunday – it was one of the few venues in London which played this regularly with live bands. The club was also a destination point for many people travelling from the North.

The club attracted many established musicians as well as new artists and bands (who cut their teeth with live performances). UK stars ranged from Maxi Priest, the late Jean Adebambo, Caroll Thompson and Janet Kay, to bands such as Loose Ends, Aswad and Five Star. Jamaican, African and US artists included Freddie McGregor, Gregory Isaacs, John Holt, Arrow, Edwin Starr, Karl Douglas, The Platters, Stylistics and Hugh Masekela. DJs such as Jazzy B and Rick Clarke learnt the ropes at Dougie's.

Soon after the club was opened, it attracted celebrities and sporting personalities. Regular visitors included Lennox Lewis, Frank Bruno, Nigel Benn, Lloyd Honeyghan, Ricky Hill, and Rudolph Walker of *EastEnders* fame. During its heyday, Mohammed Ali and the West Indies cricket team (including the likes of Clive Lloyd, Sir Vivian Richards and Gordon Greenidge) would come to the club when in Britain.

Dougie's was viewed as a club for mature and sophisticated ravers who saw this as a solace and provided escapism away from the day-to-day issues of racism, discrimination and economic recession. Dougie's, as well as other clubs such as All Nations, Mingles and Night Moves, became a fertile place for meeting people. This probably led to an explosion of long-term relationships and

2013 update:
Following a change of ownership, planning permission was granted for changes to the historic fabric of the building which, at the time of writing, stands empty and neglected.

Far left: The Kenning Hall Cinema and White Hart Pub, 1965.

Above: An original detail – a CCT monogram – from the time when it was the Clapton Cinematograph Theatre, 2009.

weddings as well as a mini-baby boom with children being born to the tune of Jean Adebambo's *Paradise*.

In 2000 Douglas retired to the Caribbean and sold Dougie's to Admiral Ken – a club owner whose West End club was able to attract artists and celebrities such as Stevie Wonder, Ben E King, Jimmy Cliff and Tom Jones. Admiral Ken renamed the club Palace Pavilion, and although he continued to run the club in a similar vein – with 'revival' dances and soca music – the growth in urban music (dancehall, hip hop, and drum and bass) attracted a new generation.

Next door the Chimes Bar, another club which had a strong youth focus, began to attract rival gangs linked to drug and street crime who saw these clubs as a place to settle scores. It was only a matter of time before the Palace Pavilion was caught up in this new environment. The tipping point was the murder of teenager Barrington Williams-Samuels in January 2006 as he sat in a car on the Lower Clapton Road opposite the Palace Pavilion.

Palace Pavilion, once a cinema and the pride and joy of the black community, became a symbol of the failure of the owner and the police to protect law-abiding clubbers and the neighbourhood from the onslaught of indiscriminate shootings. The local community, who were shocked and appalled by the escalating level of violence on the streets, had witnessed a string of murders

Above: Dougie's – Dine & Dance, 1983.

dating back to 1997 when Guy-Dance Dacres, a student, was shot dead at a private party in the Chimes Bar. The community succeeded in closing down Chimes and were finally able, in partnership with the police, to have the licence of the Palace Pavilion withdrawn – a decision upheld by the courts on appeal in January 2007.

For a variety of reasons all of the nightclubs that were part of the lovers rock, reggae and rare groove scene in Hackney have now closed. They have either been demolished, or redeveloped into new music venues or private housing. The same is true of the many cinemas to be found in Clapton, as well as in other parts of the borough. Currently the building is vacant and its future is uncertain.

As the building's centenary approaches in 2010, the Friends of Clapton Cinematograph Theatre is campaigning for the historic fabric of the cinema to be restored and brought back into community use as a cinema and educational facility. The cultural significance of the building – in the history of cinema, music and black people in Britain – needs to be recorded, preserved and celebrated in any future plans.

Patrick Vernon interviewed Mr Irvine Douglas, Admiral Ken and Mavis Gaza for the history of Dougie's and the Palace Pavilion. He would like to thank them for their contribution.

Amy Erickson

Pond House

Lower Clapton Road E5

Architect unknown *c.*1800 | listed Grade II* | on 'Buildings at Risk' register (condition – poor)

Pond House was built around 1800, when Clapton was in the fashionable, semi-rural commuter belt for London. The Lower Clapton Road was then lined with many late-Georgian detached villas. Beyond the gardens, to the east were open fields to South Mill Field before the Hackney Navigation Cut, the River Lea and Hackney Mashes.

Pond House overlooks Clapton Pond and is flanked by two older buildings: the 17th-century Bishop Wood's Almshouses to the north (Clapton's oldest building) and to the south two late 18th-century four-storey terrace houses (part of the once more extensive St James' Terrace). These buildings, together with Clapton Pond and St James' Church, form a conservation area that was established in 1971.

While the almshouses and the terrace houses adjoining are in good condition, Pond House is a mere shadow of its former glory. A two-storey stucco villa with a semicircular central portico and curved wings leading to a stable block on the north side, Pond House is Listed Grade II*, but has been on English Heritage's 'Buildings at Risk' register for about a decade. Most passers-by probably do not even notice it. Until recently it was obscured behind trees, parked cars, a dilapidated front wall, peeling paint and crumbling stonework. Currently it is completely hidden behind an enormous white fence following a fire at the house.

Approach more closely and you will discover the timber-fluted Doric columns on the raised Portland stone porch, the central double door with lions' heads mounted on circular medallions, wrought-iron railings, stone cornices and bucranium (carved ox skulls common in Classical architecture) flanking the doors in the curved wings. The back of the house, visible from

Above: Pond House before it was squatted and boarded-up, 2008.

141

Mildenhall Road, has a full three-storey semi-circular central bay.

Inside, the entrance hall, with black slate square decoration and the main staircase in the same stone, is a stunning, practically complete example of late Georgian design according to Butler & Hegarty Architects' conservation report. The staircase has its original, elaborate, wrought iron balustrade with mahogany hand rails. The first- and second-floor room arrangement is generally as originally laid out. The four principal rooms on the first floor have marble fireplaces with cornices, doors, window shutter boxes and shutters. The rear staircase has a fine balustrade and handrail.

It must have once been very grand. The front boundary wall had piers at either end with large coping stones decorated with a Greek key design. There are some 20 flues in the chimney stacks. In the cellar there is a vaulted wine store with original stone shelves and divisions, and a flag floor. The rear garden (125 metres long) had an avenue of trees, a lawn and glasshouses, which can be seen in early photographs. There was a garden room or orangery at the back of the stable block, and the original glass double doors with a decorated fanlight was still intact in 2001.

There is no record of who designed the building or for whom the house was built originally. It was probably built to a basic plan and derived by craftsmen from pattern books in a neo-classical style.

In the later 19th century the land between Lower Clapton Road and the River Lea was developed and many of the large villas on Lower Clapton Road were demolished to provide access roads. Pond House survived and was used as a house up to about c.1900, at the time that Clapton Pond itself was laid out in a 'picturesque' style. Like many large villas in Hackney, Pond House was then used briefly as a clothing factory before it passed in 1939 to the Hackney Volunteers' Social Club, made up of men who were volunteers in the Hackney Rifle Regiment. In 2000, the club membership was approximately 100, and the house was used as a meeting house. It had a club room with a bar, a committee meeting room, a large social space, snooker hall, office, steward's flat and garden. There is still an HVSC sign next to the front door.

The structure of the house has been seriously neglected over the last century. The lack of investment in the fabric of the building may have helped with its preservation and the survival of much of the historic fabric, but some repair works to the roof and windows – carried out without Listed Building Consent – have been detrimental. The materials, building techniques, form and moulding profiles used for repairs are unsympathetic and in some cases present a threat to the building. In 1954 the HVSC added a single-storey rear extension with no thought for materials or design. At the front, the steps to the porch have been rebuilt in concrete with a crude modern handrail. The stucco has been repaired to erase the original incised lines, and the decorative frieze has been covered over by a curved timber fascia. The stable block on the north side of the house, which later became the snooker room, is rotting.

Far left: Pond House, 1945.

Above: The Orangery at the back of the Stable Block, c.1880.

The fabric of the house was seen as "very vulnerable" in 2001, "and vast amounts of historic material could be destroyed by neglect in the next five years". Since then, the house was sold by HVSC to the developers Dellmount Estates. They planned to convert the house and stables into flats, and build more flats to the rear. In May 2009 Hackney Council advised the owners to withdraw and resubmit more appropriate plans.

Pond House is an exceptionally fine and practically intact historic building which, if properly and carefully restored, could be a major asset not only to its owners but to the local community. It is a significant building in the historic development of both Hackney and London, and every effort should be made to ensure its future protection. Clapton Pond Neighbourhood Action Group have, in collaboration with LBH Parks Department, successfully restored Clapton Pond. Together with the Clapton Conservation Areas Advisory Committee, this residents' group is campaigning for the house to be sympathetically repaired and restored.

2013 update:
Ann Robey has identified the person who had Pond House built for him in 1803. The erratic fortunes of Benjamin Walsh, a City stockbroker, are recounted in *Hackney: An Uncommon History in Five Parts,* published by the Hackney Society in 2012. Renovation work has begun within the house, provisionally to be completed by November 2013.

Above: Pond House, 2008.

Main: Back view, c.1890.

Elizabeth Robinson

St Mary of Eton Church

Eastway E9

Architects Bodley & Garner 1890-2 | listed Grade II

" The Mission is a queer mixture of religion, sport and social service. But the aim is never in doubt. It is to help the people of Hackney Wick to Heaven; and if they are not interested in Heaven, to help them to make the best of this life, anyway." *The Story of the Eton Mission* 1951.

St Mary of Eton is located in the easternmost part of the borough, sandwiched unpromisingly between the Blackwall Tunnel approach road, the North London Railway line and near to the River Lee Navigation, the Regent's Canal and the Olympic Park. Many people visiting the 2012 Olympics by train will pass by the south side of the church, with its striking red brick and Bath stone exterior. Yet, turn off the road, and linger for a while. Passing through the archway below the west tower, you enter a quadrangle like that of an Oxbridge college. Why is this impressive building here?

The area of Hackney Wick changed hugely in the late 19th century. A glance at the 1870 Ordnance Survey map reveals that the site the church now occupies was a ropery. To the north, there were fields and occasional buildings with idyllic-sounding names such as 'Hillyfield Cottages'. Slightly further east were the beginnings of industry, located there for the convenient proximity of the canals: dye-works; india rubber, tar and chemical works; and starch, iron, blood manure and gelatine factories. To the east and west were the beginnings of terraced housing which rapidly spread all over Hackney Wick to accommodate industrial workers. To the south was Victoria Park. Clarnico peppermint creams came a bit later. Today, the area is in the midst of another seismic change as a large swathe of land directly to the east of the church is developed as the site for the London Olympics in 2012.

The name of St Mary of Eton offers obvious clues to its history and distinctive architecture. Many public schools and Oxbridge colleges established

Above: Interior view towards the altar, c.1892.

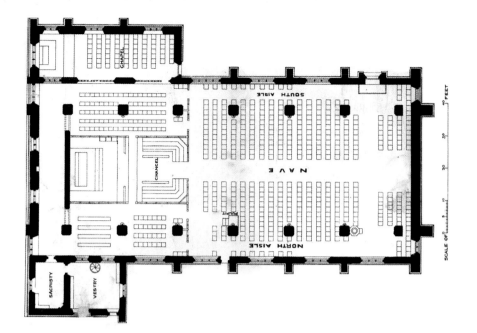

missions in deprived parts of London in the late 19th century, another example nearby being St Barnabas Church, Homerton (Charles Reilly, 1909-11), built for Merchant Taylors' School's missionary work. Eton College began its work in Hackney Wick in 1880 at the suggestion of William Walsham How, Bishop of Bedford and suffragan bishop for East London.[1]

The site for St Mary of Eton was given to the mission by a friend of Bishop How. A temporary iron church was erected there in 1881, and by 1888 Eton was fund-raising for a permanent building to designs by G. F. Bodley. All the money was raised by boys and Old Etonians. The church was consecrated on 18 June 1892. It was enlarged in 1912 to designs by Cecil Hare, who inherited Bodley's architectural practice following the latter's death in 1907. The link with Eton College continued until 1965.

On Eastway, ancillary buildings and the church form a crescendo of three gabled ends. Beginning from the south with the mission's Working Men's Club (A E Street, 1887-93) the buildings continue with the side chapel and chancel (Bodley & Garner) and culminate in the tower over the archway (Cecil Hare 1910-2). The banded red brick and stone is reminiscent of Oxbridge late 15th-century colleges.

Bodley, the leading exponent of the Perpendicular style in late Victorian architecture, was an entirely appropriate choice of architect, given Eton's origins in the mid-15th century. Entering the courtyard, the church is on the left, and to the right, the Eton Mission Buildings. Straight ahead is Eton House, designed as a homage to the buildings of Eton College. Originally a home for the mission's clergy and accommodation for Eton boys coming to Hackney to work for the mission at weekends,

this was converted into housing association flats in 1987.

Crossing the threshold into the church interior is a striking experience – a soaring, holy space. It is reminiscent of Bodley & Garner's earlier St Augustine, Pendlebury (near Manchester) built in 1871, another church in a working-class area where the architects, amidst humble surroundings, created something sublime and uplifting. At St Mary of Eton, it is the height of the nave and the purity of the plain, unadorned piers which impress.

The collegiate feel of the group of buildings can be compared with James Brooks' St Columba in Kingsland Road (now Christ Apostolic Church) of 1867-71, another of Hackney's impressive churches.

This is without doubt one of Hackney's major buildings, now in need of some renovation. Its remarkable and fine architecture stands out in an area which has suffered from largely low-quality redevelopment in recent decades.

At present, a scheme is under discussion to renovate the church, with revenue being generated by building c.30 flats. This will be achieved by converting the Mission Hall to the north, and demolishing both the Working Men's Club to the south and Verger's Cottage to the north. These two demolished buildings would be replaced by blocks of flats which would obliterate the rhythm of gables and tower on Eastway, and the shape, height and architectural style of the proposed new blocks themselves would considerably compromise the setting of the church. To bring flats onto the site is entirely right, but it is hard not to conclude that the architecture could be handled in a manner much more sympathetic to Bodley's superb design.

2013 update:
As St Mary's is rated as a 'C' priority case, it is suffering from 'slow decay' with 'no solution agreed'.

Far left: View of St Mary of Eton Church from the site of the Trowbridge Estate, 1966.

Above left: Plan of church, c.1892.

Above: View from the collegiate-like internal courtyard. The completed Trowbridge Estate can be seen in the background, 1970.

David Solman

Sight of Eternal Life Church

Shrubland Road E8

Architect Messrs Tupper and Company 1858 | listed Grade II | on 'Buildings at Risk' register
(condition – fair)

With a shimmering quadrangular steeple, distinctive lancet windows and simple corrugated shell, the Sight of Eternal Life Church is believed to be the oldest surviving example of an 'iron church' in the world.

Built in 1858 this church, affectionately known as a 'tin tabernacle', was completed in just ten weeks. Fate has been kind to it. For, unlike the majority of such buildings, there has never been sufficient money or desire to replace it with a 'permanent' building in stone or brick. Moreover, it escaped wartime damage and post-war reconstruction.

Though an inexpensive mission building, the interior is a delight. Its iron roof trusses with decorated Gothic spandrels, wooden rafters, reading platform with twisted balusters, pulpit, large church organ, and wooden pews are all bathed in natural light captured through its partially coloured east- and west-facing windows.

This building must surely rank as one of the more unashamed "industrial imposters" – a term used by A W N Pugin and many other Victorian critics of such (largely) non-conformist departures from tradition. And there have been plenty of such critics in our own time too. The Oxford English Dictionary still defines 'tin tabernacle' as a term "applied disparagingly to buildings (esp. non-conformist churches) made partly of corrugated iron".

Buildings made from a material that provides shelter for millions in the poorest cities of the world might be dismissed as of little architectural or historical interest, but such negative perceptions are changing. In recent years two books champion corrugated iron buildings. *Corrugated Iron: Building on the Frontier* by Adam Mornement and Simon Holloway (2007), and *Tin Tabernacles: Corrugated Iron Mission Halls, Churches and Chapels of Britain* by Ian Smith (2004) invite

Far left: Front elevation, 2009.

Above: Shrubland Road Evangelical Church, 1972.

149

us to rethink our approach to 19th-century temporary buildings, many of which are a wonderful part of our heritage.

Corrugated iron was invented in England in 1829 by Henry Robinson Palmer (founder of the Institute of Civil Engineers). It gradually became widespread as a material that could be useful both as cladding and to make roofs with large spans that required little or no supporting columns. Gradually, whole buildings were designed and manufactured in component parts. An 'iron church' kit was shipped to Jamaica in 1844, and in 1855 the first was built in London.

The church in Shrubland Road dates from this early period – a decade or more before 'iron churches' became a recognised category in Kelly's Trade Directory. The church was proposed by an English Presbyterian congregation based in Dalston. Having no church of their own, they held meetings at Albion Hall with the enthusiastic Reverend Thomas Whyte. The timber-framed building was designed and constructed by Messrs Tupper and Company – a City of London firm with a portfolio of galvanised iron and tinned-iron products. Costing approximately £1,250, the 37 feet by 72 feet church could reportedly accommodate up to 500 people.

The beginnings of the church were not auspicious. Reverend Whyte preached for no more than six months in the first eighteen, before an untimely death in March 1860. He was laid to rest in Abney Park Cemetery. Dr Hamilton was appointed in the interim until the induction of Reverend Davison in the winter of 1860-1. On becoming an independent or Congregational chapel in 1870, albeit a poor one, the church could attract ministers from a wider area. In 1878 the church's fortunes changed. Reverend Thomas Udall, with the assistance of his wife, firmly established the church as a focal point in the local community. For him the chapel in Shrubland Road was his calling.

During his lifetime, Udall is known to have successfully promoted the construction of at least one other 'iron church', at Twyford in Berkshire. It is certainly tempting to see Udall as a critical figure in the history of the church, putting his fundraising energies into establishing charitable services and foregoing a permanent building. He established a Sickness and Provident Society for male members of the church, built up the Sunday school roll to over 300 children, and coordinated Band of Hope meetings (a temperance organisation) for 250 children. He remained loyal to this place until his death in 1908. Today a memorial to Udall and his family can be found in

Above: Lancet window, 2009.

Abney Park Cemetery, along with many other non-conformist ministers of the period.

Udall's death was not the only challenge facing the chapel in the years before the First World War. The *Hackney and Kingsland Gazette* in 1909 reported: "The church requires a new roof and heating apparatus, and sanitary and general repairs, involving a total outlay of £400. Such a sum cannot be raised in the poor neighbourhood in which the church is situated."

Donations must have been secured, for the church was still thriving in the 1950s according to a vivid account given by a former member of the congregation in a recent Greater London Industrial Archaeology newsletter. "At the time it was heated by two huge, noisy and not particularly effective boilers; the chapel offering activities including Girls' Life Brigade and Bible Study evenings, all well attended. Moreover, it acted as a sort of marriage bureau where couples met their future spouses at, say, Band Practice."

In 1971 the church's congregation joined the nearby Hampden Chapel in Lauriston Road, and the premises at Shrubland Road became used by the evangelical Sight of Eternal Life Church. In recognition of its status as "an early, rare and complete example of an iron mission church" the building was listed Grade II by English Heritage in July 1997.

Though 'complete' in the sense of possessing both an interior and exterior of architectural and historical interest, the church's condition is less than perfect. The original tinned or galvanised iron cladding had been replaced by corrugated asbestos; and the once well-kept gardens with the original enclosure are now forlorn grounds behind a modern brick wall. But these can be put right, and there are grounds for hoping they will be: the listed status and inclusion in the Central and South Hackney Conservation Area should assure its future.

2013 update:
The church is up for sale as a family home.

John Turner

Space Studios
(formerly known as LBH Training Centre for Adults with Learning Disabilities)
Morning Lane E9

Architect Stillman Eastwick-field *c*.1960s | threatened with demolition

In 1959 the Mental Health Act devolved care for the mentally ill to local authorities and in 1963 the Department of Health published a Building Note encouraging the provision of local training centres and setting out the standards and financial allowances available. In the following year Hackney Council began work on the construction of a Training Centre for Adults with Learning Disabilities at 205a Morning Lane.

By the 1960s, Hackney Council, like most local authorities, had recruited teams of architects to deliver the very large housing, education and health building programmes which were in train. Many of the brightest students emerging from the Architectural Association, the Bartlett, Liverpool and other schools had been attracted not only by the volume of work, but – for those on the left – a commitment to public sector building programmes. And this was matched by a new architecture. In 1955, only half a mile away on

Hartlake Road, the LCC Architects' Department had built Vaine House and Granard House in a style, which – though it clearly had its origins in the work of Le Corbusier in France – was to become identified with local authorities in Britain.

The style was defined by the historian Reyner Banham in his essay *The New Brutalism* in 1955 as "memorabitilty as an image, the clear expression of structure and valuation of the materials as found". Such buildings were characterised by concrete frames struck from carefully selected boards, exposed brick and timber panels, metal windows and patent glazing. The supposed economy achieved by stripping away redundant finishes and decoration and the clear relation of the form to the use of the building, rather than any stylistic stereotype, appealed to public sector bodies operating within closely prescribed budgets. In practice the supposed savings were not always realised. The care in detailing and

Above: Front elevation, 2009.

151

NO SMOKING

FRIXOS PAPANTONIOU

8

manufacture, and the high quality of materials required to achieve the required standard, often offset any cost efficiencies. Buildings designed to fit an expected pattern of use too often became a straitjacket, as uses evolved or changed.

This era was short lived. By 1975 the then Minister of State, Anthony Crosland, had announced that for local government the party was over, and major building programmes came to an end. The oil crisis had dramatically changed the costs of running and maintaining buildings, deterioration was in some cases rapid and the Brutalist style had become an embarrassment. Though on the West Coast of America, Brutalist architecture might be associated with the houses and apartments of the very wealthy, in Britain it had become identified with the poorest social housing, welfare and other public institutional design.

By 1970 the Training Centre had closed but Hackney Social Services continued to occupy 205a Morning Lane until 1999 when it was leased to Space Studios, an arts charity that continues to manage the building as workspace for artists in East London. Though the building suffers the limitations of short-lease use and consequent lack of investment in maintenance and repair, it remains complete and largely unspoiled – and a model of public sector architecture of the 1960s.

Brutalism hardly seems the right word to describe a building that is well proportioned, meticulously detailed and surprisingly light and elegant. Though Banham believed that this new style had stripped away "the cultural dead weight of Palladio and Alberti", 205a Morning Lane – with its concrete edge beams, escape stairs and flues, projecting glazed lift and stair tower (with the affectation of opening lights distinguished in a different colour), red brick panels and eau-de-nil spandrels – is as formal an assembly of architectural elements as any Palladian villa. The style had already become a vocabulary that could be applied by a wide variety of agencies to a wide variety of buildings.

Far left: Interior showing sliding doors, 2009.

Above left: Patent glazing on tubular frames lights the ground-floor workshops, 2009.

Above: Looking east from Link Street, 1966.

2013 update:
The studios have been demolished.

Appendix I

Awards given to buildings featured in the 'Modern' chapter:

Adelaide Wharf
Building Magazine, Housing Project of the Year 2009
Civic Trust Awards, Housing 2009
Planning Awards, Best New Place to Live 2009
Building for Life Awards 2008
Hackney Design Awards 2008
Housing Design Awards 2008
RIBA Awards, London 2008
World Architecture Festival (commendation) 2008

Doris's Place
RIBA Awards, London (short-listed) 2000

Hothouse
Civic Trust Award 2009
RIBA Awards, London 2009
Hackney Design Awards 2008
BURA Awards, Best Practice in Regeneration 2004
English Partnerships Awards, Partnership in Regeneration 2004
GLA London Planning Awards 2003

In-Between
Hackney Design Awards 2004

Mossbourne Community Academy
Civic Trust Awards 2006
RIBA Awards, London 2005
Hackney Design Awards 2004

Rivington Place
Hackney Design Awards (commendation) 2008
RIBA Awards, London 2008
South Bank Show Award 2007

Rowe Lane
RIBA Awards, London 2009
Wood Awards (short-listed) 2007
Hackney Design Awards 2006

Clapton Portico Learning Centre
Hackney Design Awards, Conservation (commendation) 2006

Hackney Empire
Civic Trust Awards (commendation) 2006
RIBA Conservation Awards (commendation) 2005
US Institute of Theatre Technology Awards (merit) 2005
Hackney Design Awards 2004
Royal Fine Art Commission Building of the Year Awards, Conservation 2004

Shoreditch Town Hall
Hackney Design Awards, Conservation (commendation) 2006

Appendix II

English Heritage (EH) and Heritage Lottery Fund (HLF) grants awarded to restoration projects, 1994 -2009:

1994

12-20 Mare Street – £3313 (EH)
183 Stoke Newington High Street – £6333 (EH)
Clapton Park United Reformed Church – £232 969 (EH)
Clissold House – £58 504 (EH)
Homerton High Street – £18 990 (EH)
The Round Chapel – £349 210 (EH)
St Andrew's Church – £92 449 (EH)
St John the Baptist Church – £132 260 (EH)
Springfield Mansion – £29 557 (EH)

1995

4 Stamford Grove – £1395 (EH)
404-422 Mare Street – £3475 (EH)
Abney Park Cemetery – £3937 (EH)
Hackney Empire – £200 000 (EH)
Hoxton Hall – £11 868 (EH)
St Leonard's Church – £19 627 (EH)
St Thomas's Archway – £5152 (EH)

1996

126 Hoxton Street – £5632 (EH)
Congress Hall – £2792 (EH)
St Columba's Church – £19 450 (EH)
St Mary's Old Church – £27 000 (HLF)
Stoke Newington Boundary Scheme – £34 500 (HLF)

1997

33-39 Clissold Road – £15 998 (EH)
Clapton Square – £294 700 (HLF)
Hackney Empire – £2857 (EH)
Kingsland Road – £9811 (EH)
New Lansdowne Club – £16 215 (EH)
St John the Baptist Church – £815 730 (HLF)
St Mary of Eton Church – £6851 (EH)

1998

Holy Trinity Church (Dalston) – £38 500 (HLF)
Holy Trinity Church (Hoxton) – £12 100 (HLF)
Kingsland Road Conservation Area Partnership Scheme – £630 000 (HLF)
Pond House – £5500 (EH)
St Leonard's Church – £941 800 (HLF)

1999

37 Clissold Road – £4000 (EH)

2000

Albion Square – £46 500 (HLF)
Geffrye Museum – £50 000 (HLF)
Holy Trinity Church (Hoxton) – £59 400 (HLF)
St Andrew's Church – £1750 (EH)
St Anne with St Columba's Church – £61 600 (HLF)
St Barnabas Church – £38 550 (EH)
St Chad's Church – £51 377 (EH)

St John of Jerusalem – £31 020 (EH)
St John the Baptist – £20 600 (HLF)

2001

St John the Baptist Churchyard – £3750 (EH)
St Mark's Church – £78 000 (EH)
St Mark's Vicarage – £15 600 (EH)

2002

232 Mare Street – £24 299 (EH)
Clapton Holy Trinity with St Mary Church – £64 300 (HLF)
St Barnabas Church – £121 000 (HLF)
St John-at-Hackney – £85 400 (HLF)

2003

Clapton Pond – £5000 (EH)
Hackney Empire – £4 580 650 (HLF)
Shoreditch Town Hall – £650 000 (HLF)

2004

St Augustine's Tower – £231 000 (HLF)
St John-at-Hackney Church – £85 400 (EH)
St John-at-Hackney Churchyard Gardens – £1 790 000 (HLF)

2005

The Egerton Road Trust – £62 000 (HLF)
Geffrye Museum – £412 000 (HLF)
Hackney Downs Baptist Church – £74 000 (HLF)
New Synagogue – £49 000 (EH)
Regent's Canal and Hackney Road – £20 000 (EH)
St Leonard's Church – £132 456 (EH)

2006

Hoxton Hall – £5300 (EH)
St Barnabas Church – £120 000 (EH)

2007

Church of St Michael and All Angels – £53 000 (EH)
Church of St Michael and All Angels – £44 000 (HLF)
Clapton Seventh Day Adventist Church – £63 000 (HLF)
Clissold Park – £4 814 000 (HLF)
Haggerston Baths – £20 000 (EH)
St Barnabas Church – £78 000 (HLF)
St John of Jerusalem Church – £57 000 (EH)
St John of Jerusalem Church – £25 576 (HLF)
St Paul's Church – £63 000 (EH)

2008

St Leonard's Church – £217 000 (EH)
St Mark's Church – £74 000 (EH)

2009

Church of St Michael and All Angels – £6000 (EH)
Down's Baptist Church – £222 000 (EH)
Hoxton Hall – £93 000 (EH)

Appendix III

Buildings that have been demolished since 1960:

The Atlas Works, Berkshire Road E9 (built 1863; demolished 1989)

Bishopsgate Station and Goods Yard (built 1840; demolished 2004-5)

Clapton Federation Synagogue, Lea Bridge Road, E5 (built 1931; demolished 2006)

Clapton Stadium, Mildenhall Road E5 (built 1928; demolished 1980s)

Dalston Theatre, Dalston Lane E8 (built 1897; demolished 2007)

E Gibbons, Amhurst Road E8 (built 1890; demolished 2003)

Eastern Fever and Smallpox Hospital, Homerton Row E9 (built 1869-71; demolished 1982)

Eton Manor Boys' Club, Riseholme Street E9 (built 1913; demolished 1967)

Hackney Free and Parochial School, Chatham Place E9 (built 1811; demolished 1969)

Hackney Pavilion, Mare Street E8 (built 1913; demolished 1972)

Hackney Stadium, Waterden Road E9 (built 1932; demolished 2003)

Latham's Timber Yard, Mount Pleasant Hill E5 (built c.1911; demolished c.2003)

The Mothers' Hospital, Lower Clapton Road E5 (built 1913; demolished 1987)

Nichols Square, off Hackney Road E2 (built 1841; demolished 1962)

Our Lady's Wing – St Joseph's Hospice, Cambridge Heath Road E8 (built 1956; demolished 2002)

The Pilkington Works, Shepherdess Walk N1 (built 1930-1; demolished c.1970)

Pitfield Street Baths and Washhouses, Pitfield Street N1 (built 1899; demolished 1962-3)

St John the Evangelist, Queen's Drive N4 (built 1869-78; demolished c.1991)

The Flying Scud Public House, Hackney Road E2 (built c.1860s; demolished 2009)

Spurstowe's Almshouses, Sylvester Path E8 (built 1689; demolished 1966)

Trowbridge Estate, Hackney Wick E9 (built 1965-9; demolished 1985 onwards)

Victoria and Albert Cottages, Myrtleberry Street E8 (built c.1860; demolished c.1970s)

Victoria Park Lido, Victoria Park E9 (built 1934; demolished 1990)

Woodberry Down Comprehensive School, Woodberry Down Estate N4 (built 1950-6; demolished 1999)

Appendix IV

Buildings on English Heritage's 'Building at Risk' register 2009:

Commercial

The Griffin Public House, Leonard Street, EC2 (Grade II)

Educational

Testi and Sons Millwrights, Waterworks Lane, E5 (Grade II)

Industrial

Cleeve Workshops, Calvert Avenue, E2 (Grade II)

Hackney Borough Disinfecting Station, Millfields Road, E5 (Grade II)

Walls and gates to Bishopsgate Goods Station, Shoreditch High Street, E1 (Grade II)

Public

Air Raid Precaution Centre, Rossendale Street, E5 (Grade II)

Court House and Police Station, Old Street, EC1 (Grade II)

Haggerston Baths, Whiston Road, E2 (Grade II)

Religious

Monuments at Abney Park Cemetery, Stoke Newington High Street, N16 (Grade II)

Chapel at Abney Park Cemetery, Stoke Newington High Street, N16 (Grade II)

Abney Park Cemetery, Stoke Newington High Street, N16 (Grade II)

St Andrew's Church, Bethune Road, N16 (Grade II*)

St Columba's Vicarage and link to church, Kingsland Road, E2 (Grade I)

St Barnabas Church, Shacklewell Lane, E8 (Grade II*)

St Leonard's Church, Shoreditch High Street, E2 (Grade I)

Walls and gates to St Leonard's Churchyard, Shoreditch High Street, E1 (Grade II)

Sight of Eternal Life Church, Shrubland Road, E8 (Grade II)

Residential

Bishop Wood's Almshouses, Lower Clapton Road, E5 (Grade II)

7 Clapton Square, E5 (Grade II)

55 and 59 Clapton Terrace, N16 (Grade II)

Clissold House, N16 (Grade II*)

Marlow House, 160 Dalston Lane, E8 (Grade II)

320 Kingsland Road, E8 (Grade II)

592 Kingsland Road, E8 (Grade II)

Forecourt wall to Pond House, 162 Lower Clapton Road, E5 (Grade II)

Pond House, 162 Lower Clapton Road, E5 (Grade II*)

Stables to north of Pond House, 162 Lower Clapton Road, E5 (Grade II)

New Lansdowne Club, 195 Mare Street, E8 (Grade II*)

222 Mare Street, E8 (Grade II)

276 Queensbridge Road, E8 (Grade II)

187 Shoreditch High Street, E2 (Grade II)

196 Shoreditch High Street, E2 (Grade II)

91 Stoke Newington Church Street, N16 (Grade II)

White Lodge, Springfield Park, E5 (Grade II)

Endnotes

The Round Chapel (pp 69-71)

1. The URC was formed in 1981 by the merger of the Congregationalists and the Presbyterian Church of England and Wales.

Clapton Federation Synagogue (pp 92-5)

1. I am grateful to architect Hedy Parry-Davies for first bringing Glass's work to my attention in her dissertation 'Synagogues in England – A Heritage under threat?' Architectural Association, London, May 1998 (post-graduate Diploma in Building Conservation).

2. In the 1983 edition, *Buildings of England: County Durham,* 2nd edn., p 452.

3. Geoffrey Alderman, *The Federation of Synagogues,* London 1987, p 62.

4. *Jewish Cronicle* (JC) 30 Oct. 1931.

5. *JC* 10 June 1932.

6. 7 March 1887 Old Style. He died on 31 January 1932.

7. Obituary *RIBA Journal* 19 Feb. 1932, p 440. Genealogical information, personal testimony and copies of vital records kindly provided by his daughter Denise Williams (b.1923), née Glass, London, 20 Sep. 2006.

8. Arnold Levy, *History of the Sunderland Jewish Community,* London, 1956, pp 145-7. The original architect's description and a sketch plan of the proposed building have been traced in Tyne & Weir Archives C/SU74. I have seen the actual plans: Plan no. 269/5777-5788 (103), 'Proposed Synagogue & Hall, Ryhope Road, Sunderland, for the Sunderland Hebrew Congregation'. Signed 'M.K.Glass, FRIBA; Architect, 20 Saville Row, Newcastle-on-Tyne', not dated but refers to letter dated. 30 Aug. 1927. Also *JC* 23 March, 14 Dec. 1928; *The Brick Builder* March 1931, p 19.

9. Obituary *JC* 12 Feb. 1932.

10. Ironically, it is the unlisted Jesmond, Eskdale Terrace in Newcastle that now seems to have the best chance of survival. Closed in 1986, it found a new use as the Central Newcastle High School for Girls and has been sympathetically restored – although sadly the interior is lost.

Eton Manor Boys' Club (pp 96-9)

1. *The Times,* 8 March 1969.

2. Barnett, *Practical Socialism,* p 26, 1898.

3. LSE Charles Booth online B346 pp168-170.

4. RIBA CoRo/1/1 Diary of Rose Ellen Cooper (Goodhart-Rendel's mother), Feb. 1913; other early works include the Pantiles in Englefield Green, Surrey (1911) and cottages at East and West Clandon in West Horsley (1909-13).

Nichols Square (pp 106-9)

1. He was the first gardener to understand the process of plant reproduction and to use artificial scientific hybridisation to create new species. His hybrid flower 'Fairchild's Mule' was a cross between a sweet william and a carnation.

2. According to H M Colvin, the architect John Henry Taylor exhibited at the Royal Academy from 1827 to 1841, and was one of a committee formed in 1834 that established the Institute of British Architects. He designed St Anne's Society Schools, Brixton Hill (1829); The Albany Chapel, Hampstead Road (1835); All Saint's, Sidmouth; the infirmary of the Infant Orphan Asylum, Wanstead (1854).

3. LMA GLC/AR/HB/02/3450.

4. LMA MA/SC/L/427.

5. LMA GLC/AR/HB/02/3450.

6. Newspaper cutting from 1962 in LMA GLC/AR/HB/02/3450.

7. They recommended that the LCC's Historic Buildings Section should make adequate records for the Survey of London.

8. Elizabeth Robinson, *Lost Hackney,* 1989, p 20.

Nicholl House (pp 134-6)

1. Information from English Heritage Historian's file, report by Andrew Saint, dated 1994. See also the *Official Architect,* May 1946, pp 260-3, which shows a model of the eight-storey flats, as part of an exhibition entitled 'Building Now' at the Royal Institute of British Architects.

2. 'Ossulton Street: Early LCC Experiments in High-Rise Housing, 1925-29', Simon Pepper, *The London Journal,* vol. 7 no. 1 Summer, 1981, pp 54-55. Similarities have also been drawn with the Quarry Hill Estate Leeds (1933-5) and Bruno Taut's Hufeisin Seidlung at Britz, Berlin (1925-30).

3. See *Architect's Journal,* March 3, 1949, p209: *Architect & Building News,* February, 1935, pp 163-4, which refers to their unusual construction.

4. Op cit: Andrew Saint.

St Mary of Eton Church (pp 145-7)

1. "By 1887, at least sixteen schools and colleges were taking entire or partial responsibility for Church of England missions in working-class parts of London…Such help relieved clergymen of financial worry, and often provided them with the personal service of earnest young laymen. Some – like the Eton Mission in Hackney Wick – were intended to remain missions permanently." *Churches and the Working Classes in Victorian England*, by K S Inglis (1963).

Contributors

Allen Abramson is a social anthropologist and senior lecturer at University College London. He spent over two years in Western Polynesia researching cultural aspects of social life in Fijian chiefdoms. He is currently researching the cultural significance of extreme practice in late-modern societies and has recently published articles on cliff jumping, rock-climbing and outdoor training courses. He has climbed on both real and synthetic rock since 1981. He has lived in Hackney since 1988.

Geraldine Bedell is a journalist at the *Observer,* and a writer of fiction and non-fiction. Her publications include *The Handmade House: A Love Story Set in Concrete* (2005) and *The Gulf Between Us* (2009). She lives in London with her husband and four children.

Monica Blake is a library and information consultant. She was a member of the Save the Reservoirs Campaign from 1987 until it disbanded in 2006. She also edited the Campaign's newsletter from 1991. Since 1988 she has been a member of the Hackney Society (co-editor of *Spaces* since 2008, elected vice-chair in 2007). She is also a member of the Clapton Conservation Areas Advisory Committee. She has lived in Hackney since 1980.

Paul Bolding is a freelance financial journalist who spent most of his career with Reuters. He has a special interest in history and archaeology and has been a volunteer at Sutton House. He has lived in Hackney since 1989.

Heloise Brown currently works as a conservation advisor for the Victorian Society. She has lived in and around Hackney since 2004.

Chris Dorley-Brown is a photographer and filmmaker. In 1987 he started to document all of Hackney's tower blocks as the demolition programme began. In 2001 he re-shot the pictures from the same viewpoint as part of a project *Revisits 1987-2001*. This work has been shown internationally in the touring exhibition *Potential: Ongoing Archive.* A number of his photographs are held at Hackney Archives and the Museum of London. He has lived in Hackney since 1980.

Tom Dyckhoff is a writer, broadcaster and critic on architecture, cities and design. He is architecture and design critic at *The Times* and appears on BBC2's *The Culture Show.* He also writes a weekly column for the *Guardian* and teaches at the Bartlett School of Architecture, University College London. He is currently filming the series *Saving Britain's Past* to be shown on BBC2 in late 2009. He has lived all over London, but he'll never forget his time in Hackney.

Laurie Elks is a trustee of Hackney Historic Buildings Trust where he acts as the custodian of St Augustine's Tower. For many years he wound the Tower's clock (it is now done electronically). He is passionate about the Lee Valley Regional Park and was co-founder of the Lee Valley Association. He has recently written a brief history of the park authority in *Hackney History*. He is also a life member of the Hackney Society. He formerly worked as a lawyer investigating miscarriages of justice and is a founder member of the Criminal Cases Review Commission. He has lived in Hackney since 1972.

Amy Erickson is currently the chair of Hackney Parks Forum, which represents park user groups across the borough. She works for the Cambridge Group for Population History at the University of Cambridge. Most of her publications deal with feminist economic history of the 17th and 18th centuries. She has lived in Hackney since 1994.

Patrick Hammill is a divisional director at Levitt Bernstein Associates – an award-winning architectural practice based in Hackney. He is currently the chair of Hackney Historic Buildings Trust. He is also a long-standing member of the Hackney Society where initially he was the secretary and later the chair from the 1980s until circa 2003. He has lived in Hackney since 1977.

David Heath was formerly chief conservation architect at English Heritage, and is now a historic buildings consultant. From 1983 to 1987 he was part-time caseworker to the Hackney Society, during which time he worked on the following publications: *South Shoreditch: Historic and Industrial Buildings* (1986) and *Buildings at Risk in Hackney* (1987). He also contributed to *Workshops and Warehouses, a Walk around the East End Furniture Industry* (1988).

Nick Holder is an archaeologist and historian who is currently completing a PhD at Royal Holloway, University of London. He is researching the Dissolution of London's monasteries. Previously he worked for the Museum of London Archaeology Service on several large excavations. His publications include *The London Guildhall: an Archaeological History of a Neighbourhood from Early Medieval to Modern Times* (2007). He is also co-founder of Clapton Pond Neighbourhood Action Group and Shakespeare Neighbourhood Residents' Association. He lives in Hackney with his partner and son.

Tim Horsey is a freelance writer, editor and journalist who specialises in the field of property investment. His affection for Hackney dates from the 1980s when he first moved to London and lived for a number of years in Lauriston Road. These days he often cycles to work from his home in Leytonstone along the stretch of the Regent's Canal that forms the southern edge of the borough.

Sharman Kadish is director of Jewish Heritage UK and part-time lecturer in Jewish Studies at the University of Manchester. She has published widely on Anglo-Jewish history, heritage and architecture. Her most recent publications include *Jewish Heritage in England* (2006) and *Jewish Heritage in Gibraltar* (2007). She is currently preparing *The Synagogues of Britain and Ireland: an Architectural and Social History* for publication. Her father, the artist Norman Kadish (1916-1988) grew up in Lea Bridge Road.

Julia Lafferty was a staff member of the trade union ASTMS which was based at Sutton House until 1982. In 1987 she was a founder of the Save Sutton House Campaign, which later became the Sutton House Society. Currently she is the secretary of the Friends of Clapton Cinematograph Theatre, and a member of Clapton Conservation Areas Advisory Committee and Clapton Pond Neighbourhood Action Group. She lives in Hackney.

Patrick Lynch is an architect who practises with his wife Claudia. Lynch Architects work has been widely published and they won the Young Architects of the Year Award 2005-6. He has taught at the Architectural Association (2001-3), Kingston University (1997-2003) and London Metropolitan University (2005-7). Their work ranges from individual houses and residential and commercial developments to arts and community projects. He lived in Hackney for ten years, but moved over the border in 2008.

Chris Miele is a town planner and architectural historian. He published *Hoxton – Architecture and History Over Five Centuries* for the Hackney Society in 1992. He is currently editing and contributing to *Middlesex Guildhall in Parliament Square for the New UK Supreme Court* (2010). Recently he has also edited *From William Morris* (2006) a publication on the history of the conservation movement. From the mid-1990s he chaired the Clapton Conservation Areas Advisory Committee; and in 2002 co-founded the Clapton Pond Neighbourhood Action Group. He works as a chartered town planner and is a partner at Montagu Evans LLP. He lives in south London with his wife and daughter.

Kevin Moore is chief executive of Walworth Garden Farm – a charity and social enterprise that teaches horticulture and provides employment opportunities in organic gardening. He is currently chair of the Hackney Society and Central and South Hackney Conservation Areas Advisory Committee. He is also a judge for the Civic Trust Awards. In his spare time he enjoys renovating historic properties. He has lived in Hackney since 1992.

John O'Callaghan (b.1934, d.2007) was an active member of the Haggerston Pool Community Trust during his time in Hackney. He worked as a journalist for the *Guardian* and RTÉ (Ireland's public service broadcaster). Haggerston Pool Community Trust was set up by local residents in 2000 to campaign for the restoration and reopening of Haggerston Baths.

Matt Payne is a conservation officer for the Urban Design and Conservation Team at Hackney Council. His work regularly brings him into contact with the borough's many listed buildings and conservation areas. He also supports the six Conservation Areas Advisory Committees. He has a continued interest in discovering and learning about the built environment wherever he visits and is an associate member of both the Institute of Historic Building Conservation and Royal Town Planning Institute. He lives in Hackney.

Lisa Rigg is a heritage education consultant with experience of coordinating heritage and outreach projects at a local and national level. In 2004 she and a colleague became the first winners of the Roots and Wings Award for innovative heritage provision. She has also worked for the Building Exploratory, MLA London, the Campaign for Drawing, RIBA and Eastside Community Heritage. Currently she is coordinating a research and oral history project about historic hospitals in Hackney. She wrote *Exploring* *the Tower* (2006) – a teachers' resource pack about St Augustine's Tower. She also edited *The Clapton Cookbook* (2008), *Trouble at the Tower* (2009); and two walking guides *Kingsland Road – Panorama* (2002) and *Beating the Bounds of the Games in Hackney Wick* (2009). She co-founded Clapton Pond Neighbourhood Action Group in 2002. She has lived in Hackney since 1995.

Ann Robey is an economic, social and architectural historian and heritage consultant whose career includes research and writing for the Survey of London. She is co-author of *100 Years of Suburbia: The Aldersbrook Estate in Wanstead* (1999), and contributed to *Greenwich: An Architectural History of the Royal Hospital for Seamen and the Queen's House* (2000). She also wrote the *London Suburbs Report* (2008) for SAVE and ten Conservation Area Appraisals for Hackney Council. Recently she has also worked for Hackney Historic Buildings Trust where she managed the restoration of St Augustine's Tower. She is a trustee of the Hackney Society and the Heritage of London Trust.

Elizabeth Robinson is editor of *The Victorian,* the magazine of the Victorian Society. She is fascinated by the historic fabric of the area and wrote *Lost Hackney* (1989) and *Twentieth Century Buildings in Hackney* (1999), both published by the Hackney Society. She has lived in Hackney since 1983.

Ray Rogers is the head of the Urban Design and Conservation Team at Hackney Council. Before that he was a historic buildings inspector at English Heritage (London region). This followed a career in both the public and private sectors working on major conservation, planning and development schemes in London and elsewhere. He spent part of his childhood on the Woodberry Down Estate and had an aunt who taught art at Woodberry Down Secondary School.

Tim Ronalds is an architect and was one of the '4 British Architects' featured in the 9H Gallery exhibition in 1990. His practice, based in Hackney, is known for bold projects in arts and education – often for clients with social agendas. Hackney Empire is one of the best-known projects, but others include The Landmark (Devon), Mick Jagger Centre (Kent), Jackson's Lane Theatre (London) and The Circus Space (Hackney).

Joanna Smith is a building historian, working initially for the Royal Commission on the Historical Monuments of England and latterly for English Heritage. She is co-author of *Behind the Veneer: South Shoreditch – The Furniture Trade and its Buildings* (2006). She has lived in various parts of Hackney, including the Woodberry Down Estate, and has had the good fortune in having been able to record a number of its historic buildings.

David Solman is chair of the Abney Park Trust, and writes about garden history. His publications include *Loddiges of Hackney: the Largest Hothouse in the World* (1995). He works in transport planning.

Cathy Strongman is a freelance writer specialising in architecture, design and sustainability. She regularly contributes to *Elle Decoration,* the *Evening Standard, The Architects' Journal, Grand Designs* magazine and the *V&A Magazine.* She also writes a monthly eco-column for *House & Garden* magazine and has written four books including *The Sustainable Home* (2008) and *100 Houses: Modern Designs for Contemporary Living* (2009). She has also appeared as an architectural critic on ITV1. She lives in Hackney.

Vyki Sparkes coordinates historic loans for the National Museum of Science and Industry – a family of museums that includes the Science Museum. She is passionate about local history and lives in East London.

Amin Taha is director of Amin Taha Architects – which for three years running has been selected as one of Europe's 40 best young practices. It was founded in 2001 after winning two competitions including a proposed arts centre off Broadway Market. Since then the practice has designed seven residential projects including the Gazzano House, which falls inside the Rosebery Avenue Conservation Area.

Jerry Tate is principal of Jerry Tate Architects. He previously gained extensive experience of delivering large-scale commercial and sustainable projects for Grimshaw Architects including the Eden Project (Cornwall) and Paddington Station Phase 2B (London). A winner of two prestigious academic awards, the Antoine Predock Design Award and the Kevin V Kieran Award, he has taught at Harvard University and currently teaches at the Bartlett School of Architecture, University College London. His interests combine his experience of sustainable development with a knowledge of new technologies and computer software to give him a unique insight into the future of low-carbon development.

Anthony Thistleton is a director of Waugh Thistleton Architects. Their work currently includes a proposal to restore the Gaumant Cinema in Hoxton and design a new synagogue in the grounds of the Jewish cemetery in Lauriston Road. His interest in ICT and multimedia gives insight into the rapidly developing area of virtual environment design, allowing the practice to use ICT to design sustainable architecture.

John Turner was formerly head of architectural policy at the Department of Environment (now known as Defra). He currently chairs the Kingsland Conservation Areas Committee. He has lived in Hackney since 1974.

Patrick Vernon is the founder of Every Generation, an organisation that promotes black history and heritage. He created the website *100 Great Black Britons;* and produced and co-directed *A Charmed Life,* a film about the life of Eddie Noble – a Hackney resident who served in the RAF during the Second World War. Patrick is also a councillor for Queensbridge Ward and is involved in the Reclaiming Holly Street Campaign.

Suzanne Waters is a lecturer in architectural history and is currently working part-time at the RIBA Drawings Collection – cataloguing the drawings of Sir Denys Lasdun. She is member of the Hackney Society and a trustee of the Twentieth Century Society. She has lived in Hackney for over 20 years.

Isobel Watson researches and writes about London history. Among other books and articles are *Gentlemen in the Building Line: the Development of South Hackney* (1989), and *Hackney and Stoke Newington Past – a pictorial history* (2006). She has chaired the Friends of Hackney Archives since their foundation in 1985, and edits their annual journal *Hackney History.*

Margaret Willes was the Publisher to the National Trust until her retirement in 2005. Her first book, *Reading Matters: Five Centuries of Discovering Books* was published by Yale University Press in 2008, and her second, on botanical illustrations, will be published by the Bodleian Library in late 2009. She has lived in Hackney since 1982.

Sarah Wise is the author of *The Blackest Streets: The Life and Death of a Victorian Slum* (2009) – a history of the Old Nichol, which stood on the site of today's Boundary Street Estate. Her debut book *The Italian Boy: Murder and Grave Robbery in 1830s London* focuses on an area just south of Hackney Road. This was short-listed for the 2005 Samuel Johnson Prize for Non-Fiction and won the Crime Writers' Association Gold Dagger for Non-Fiction. She grew up in West London and has lived in Tottenham Court Road for nearly 20 years.

Ken Worpole is the author of many books on social history, landscape and architecture, including *Dockers and Detectives* (2008) and *Modern Hospice Design* (Routledge, 2009). He is a professor at London Metropolitan University, and is married to the photographer, Larraine Worpole. He has lived in Hackney since 1969.

Bibliography and archival sources

Hackney Archives (HA)

London Metropolitan Archives (LMA)

National Monuments Record, Swindon (NMR)

The National Archives (TNA)

St Bartholomew's Hospital Archive (SBHA)

Surrey History Centre (SHC)

Chapter 1: Modern

Adelaide Wharf

Allford Hall Monaghan Morris, Adelaide Wharf Info Pack (Allford Hall Monaghan Morris, undated).

Robey, A, Regent's Canal Draft Conservation Area Appraisal (London Borough of Hackney, 2007).

'Adelaide Wharf', www.adelaidewharf.com (accessed August 2009).

'Allford Hall Monaghan Morris', www.ahmm.co.uk/projects/done/done_adelaide_wharf.php (accessed August 2009).

'Architects' Journal', www.architectsjournal.co.uk/video-the-team-behind-adelaide-wharf/1994765.article (accessed August 2009).

'Commission for Architecture and the Built Environment', www.cabe.org.uk/case-studies/adelaide-wharf/evaluation (accessed August 2009).

Geffrye Museum extension

Dyckhoff, T, 'Nigel Coates comes in from the cool', The Times, 15 April 2008.

Glancey, J, Nigel Coates: Body Buildings and City Scapes (Thames and Hudson, 1999).

In-between

French, H, New Urban Housing (Laurence King Publishing, 2006).

Powell, K with Strongman, C (eds), 'In-Between', New London Architecture 2 (Merrell, 2007).

Whitehead, T, 'Annalie Riches, Silvia Ullmayer and Barti Garibaldo came together on In-Between', Architects' Journal, 25 November 2004.

'Inhabitat', www.inhabitat.com/index.php?s=whatcott (accessed April 2009).

Chapter 2: Restored

Clapton Portico Learning Centre

Alvey, N, 'The London Orphan Asylum, Clapton', The Terrier, Volume 21, Winter 1991.

Mander, D, An Illustrated History of Hackney (Sutton Publishing, 1998).

Mander, D and Golden, J, The London Borough of Hackney in Old Photographs 1890-1960 (Sutton Publishing, 1991).

Pidwell, S, 'Classical Revival: Brady Mallalieu's Clapton Portico', Architecture Today, Issue 166, 1 March 2006.

Robinson, E, Lost Hackney (The Hackney Society, 1989).

Robinson, W, History and Antiquities of the Parish of Hackney (J B Nichols and Sons, 1842-3).

Watson, I, Hackney and Stoke Newington Past: A Visual History of Hackney and Stoke Newington (Historical Publications, 1998).

SHC, London Orphan Asylum Annual Reports, 1821 and 1822.

HA 236P, Rohu, Brigadier H V, A Short History of the Congress Hall (1932).

HA 361.2 LON P, Historical Notes on Congress Hall, Linscott Road, The London Orphan Asylum (Greater London Council, 1971).

London Fields Lido

Robinson, E, Twentieth Century Buildings in Hackney (The Hackney Society, 1999).

Smith, J, Liquid Assets: the Lidos and Open Air Swimming Pools of Britain (English Heritage, 2005).

'Open-Air Swimming Pools or Lidos – in the United Kingdom', www.lidos.org.uk (accessed February 2009).

HA, Hackney Gazette, 27th April 1932.

HA, Hackney Gazette, 29th April 1932.

HA, Hackney Gazette, 2nd May 1932.

St Augustine's Tower

Mander, D, St John-at-Hackney: The Story of a Church (The Parish of Hackney, 1993).

The County of Middlesex, Volume 10 (Victoria County History of England, 1995).

An Inventory of the Historical Monuments in London, Volume V, East London (Royal Commission on the Historic Monuments of England, 1930).

HA, 'St. John-at-Hackney', Florence Bagust collection, Volume 15, no date.

HA CC/2/10, 'St. John's Church Tower, Hackney. Report on its condition from an inspection made in February 1932'.

HA, various historic images catalogued under 'St John-at-Hackney' and 'St Augustine's Tower'.

Shoreditch Town Hall

Cherry, B and Pevsner, N, *The Buildings of England London 4: North* (Penguin, 1998).

Rogers R and Smith, J, *Behind the Veneer: The South Shoreditch Furniture Trade and its Buildings* (English Heritage, 2006).

Smith, J, *London's Town Halls: The Architecture of Local Government from 1840 to the Present* (English Heritage and RIBA Heinz Gallery, 1999).

NMR Building File 95885, Shoreditch Town Hall.

Stoke Newington West Reservoir Centre

Cosh, M, *The New River,* 2nd edition (Islington Archaeology and History Society, 1988).

Essex-Lopresti, M, *Exploring the New River* (KAF Brewing Books, 1986).

Long, K, 'Nautical but nice', *Building Design,* 27 April 2001.

Ward, R, *London's New River* (Historical Publications, 2003).

'Reservoir alert', Hegarty, C (ed), *The Hackney Society Newsletter,* Volume 1, Number 7, Spring 1991.

'Local Voices, Local Views: a Community Consultation', Save the Reservoirs Campaign, 1992.

'Stoke Newington Water Works: The Way Forward', Thames Water, 1992.

'Commission for Architecture and the Built Environment', www.cabe.org.uk/case-studies/stoke-newington-west-reservoir-centre

(accessed May 2009).

'Marks Barfield Architects', www.marksbarfield.com/project.php?projectid=12 (accessed July 2009).

Sutton House

Belcher, V, Bond, R, Gray, M and Wittrick, A, *Sutton House – A Tudor Courtier's House in Hackney* (English Heritage, 2004).

Wright, P, *A Journey Through Ruins: The Last Days of London* (Oxford University Press, 2009).

Worship Street

Kirk, S, *Philip Webb: Pioneer of Arts and Crafts Architecture* (John Wiley and Sons, 2005).

Pevsner, N, 'Colonel Gillum and the Pre-Raphaelite Brotherhood', *The Burlington Magazine,* Volume 95, 1953.

Rogers, R and Smith, J, *Behind the Veneer: The South Shoreditch Furniture Trade and its Buildings* (English Heritage, 2006).

The Builder, 29 August 1863.

Chapter 3: Forgotten

Hackney Stadium

Fenn, C, *Hackney Speedway, Friday At Eight* (Tempus Publishing, 2003).

Gill, S, *Hackney Wick* (Nobody and the Archive of Modern Conflict, 2005).

Greyhound Racing in London (The National Greyhound Racing Society of Great Britain, 1962).

'The Wick was ramshackle, basic beast of a greyhound track…and all the better for it' http://betting.betfair.com/greyhound-racing/general 24 October 2007.

'Bankrupt on the first night – the desperate story of the new Hackney Wick' http://betting.betfair.com/greyhound-racing/lost-tracks 31 October 2007.

'Regeneration came five years too late for much-loved Hackney Wick', http://betting.betfair.com/greyhound-racing/lost-tracks 6 November 2007.

'UK Running Track Directory', www.runtrackdir.com (accessed May 2009).

'Hackney Wick Stadium (Wikipedia), http://en.wikipedia.org/wiki/Hackney_Wick_Stadium (accessed May 2009).

The Mothers' Hospital

Richardson, H (ed), *English Hospitals 1660-1948: A Survey of their Architecture and Design* (Royal Commission on the Historic Monuments of England, 1998).

SBHA SBHF/HA/1/1, *The Mothers' Hospital Annual Report,* 1911.

SBHA SBHF/HA/1/24, *The Mothers' Hospital Annual Report,* 1936.

Pitfield Street Baths and Washhouses

Mander, D, *A Hackney Century 1900-1999* (Sutton Publishing, 1999).

Miele, C, *Hoxton: Architecture and History Over Five Centuries* (The Hackney Society, 1993).

Watson, I, *Hackney and Stoke Newington Past* (Billing and Sons Ltd, 1990).

Shoreditch: The Official Guide, (ed J Burrows and Co Ltd Publishers, 1962).

The Architect, 4 May 1900.

The Building News, 13 December 1895.

The Municipal Journal of London, 1899.

HA L/V/118, Opening of Pitfield Street baths and washhouses – souvenir programme, 18 March 1899.

HA L/B/69, Competition for Baths and Library building: instructions to competing architects, March 1895.

HA L/B/71, Draft reply to questions from competitors 1895.

HA L/B/72, Bundle of envelopes containing slips identifying architects of numbered, designs submitted in the competition for the Baths and Library building, 1895.

HA L/B/73, Letter to Baths Commissioners and Library Commissioners, giving judge's decision in competition for new buildings, 26 Nov 1895.

HA L/B/75/1, Specification for the Baths, 1896-97.

HA L/B/79, Bundle of miscellaneous correspondence, 1896.

HA L/B/74, Form of Tender for erection of the Baths and Wash-houses, Pitfield Street, 1896-97.

Woodberry Down Comprehensive School

Post-War Steering Group, Woodberry Down Comprehensive School, Woodberry Down, Hackney. (English Heritage, undated).

Parker, S, 'From the Slums to the Suburbs: Labour Party Policy, the LCC, and the Woodberry Down Estate, Stoke Newington 1934-1961', *London Journal,* Volume 24, No 2, 1999.

Woodberry Down Memories Group, Woodberry Down Memories: History of a LCC Housing Estate (ILEA Education Resource Unit, 1989).

The Architects' Journal, 27 October 1949.

The Architects' Journal, 8 September 1955.

Architecture and Building, October 1955.

Official Architecture and Planning, October 1955.

The Architect and Building News, 20 October 1955.

Historic Building Report – Woodberry Down Secondary School (Royal Commission on the Historical Monuments of England, 1997).

Chapter 4: Ignored

Cleeve Workshops

Beattie, S, *A Revolution in London Housing: LCC Housing Architects and their Work 1893-1914* (Greater London Council, 1980).

Aves, E, 'The Furniture Trade' in Booth, C, *Life and Labour of the People in London,* Volume 1: East London, Part II: The Trades (Macmillan, 1902-3).

Lawson, A, *Handmade in London* (Cassell, 1978).

Rogers R and Smith, J, *Behind the Veneer: The South Shoreditch Furniture Trade and its Buildings* (English Heritage, 2006).

LMA LCC/MIN/7353, London County Council Housing of the Working Classes Committee Papers, Mar-Dec 1896.

Haggerston Baths

'Report of grand opening', *Hackney Gazette,* June 1904.

Continuum Sport and Leisure Ltd, Feasibility Study: Leisure and Swimming Facilities and Haggerston Baths Regeneration Project (London Borough of Hackney, 2006).

Cross, A W, *Public Baths and Washhouses,* 1906.

Tassell, W, *Memories of Haggerston Pool* (unpublished, 2003).

Gordon, I and Inglis, S, *Great Lengths – The Historic Indoor Swimming Pools of Great Britain* (English Heritage and Played in Britain, 2009).

Entwistle, J, *Haggerston Baths* (unpublished, 2009).

New Lansdowne Club

Benjamin, C, *Glimpses of Ancient Hackney and Stoke Newington* (1894).

Bolter, J, '195 Mare Street', *Hackney History,* Volume 12 (Friends of Hackney Archives, 2006).

HA P/J/P, Parish Ratebooks.

HA D/S/58, Fry Refuge minutes and annual reports.

TNA PROB 36/9, 18/29/33.

Nicholl House

London County Council, *Housing: A Survey of the Post War Housing Work of the London County Council 1945-1949* (London County Council, 1949).

Official Architect, May 1946.

Pepper, S, 'Ossulton Estate: Early LCC Experiments in High-Rise Housing, 1925-9', *The London Journal,* No 1, Volume 7, Summer 1981.

'Needwood House', *Architects' Journal,* 3 March 1949.

'Evelyn Court', *Architect and Building News,* February 1935.

Pond House

Butler and Hegarty Architects, Pond House report (Hackney Historic Buildings Trust/English Heritage, 2001).

'Victoria County History', www.british-history.ac.uk/report.aspx?compid=22702 (accessed May 2009).

Credits

Index

A

Abercrombie, Sir Patrick 117, 135
Abney Park:
   Cemetery 123, 155, 157
   Chapel 123
   Trust 124
Adelaide Wharf 11, **19-21**
Adjaye Associates **41-3**
Admiral Ken 140
Aish, Clifford A 101
Alexander, Nick 73
Allford Hall Monaghan Morris **19-21**
Allport, John 107
almshouses 11, 29, 141
aluminium 47, 61, 116
Art:
   Deco 95
   Nouveau 113
artists 13, 23, 33, 41, 125, 139-40, 153
Arts Council, The 65
Arts and Crafts 81
Ash Sakula Architects **32-4**
Association of Supervisory Staff,
Executives and Technicians (ASSET) 83
Atlas Works, The **86-8**
auditorium 39, 65
Autograph (ABP) 41
Avanti Architects 31
Aves, Ernest 127

B

Barings Bank 99
Barratt, E C 127
Batchelder, David 13, 97
baths, public 11, 13, 111, 113, 129-30
Beaux-Arts 31
bell-tower 73
Berkshire Road 87
Bethnal Green 23, 53, 109
Betjemen, Sir John 13
Billings, Robert 55, 57
Bishop of London 74
Bishop Wood's Almshouses 141
Bishopsgate Station and Goods Yard
   11, **89-91**
Black (ethnicity) 41, 139-40
Blair, Tony 39
Blaisse, Petra 65
blowdown 115
Bodley and Garner 145, 147
Bodley, George Frederick 147
boiler 46, 57, 68, 111, 129-30, 150
bomb damage 130, 133
Booth, Charles 109, 127
Booth, General William 61
Boundary Street Estate 11, **125-7**
Bourne, Sir Clive 39
Brady Mallalieu Architects **59-61**
Braithwaite Viaduct 89, 91
Branson Coates **25-7**
British Xylonite Company 87
Broadway Market 14, 19, 23
Bronco 87-8
Brooke House 74
Brooke Simpson Spiller 88
Brutalism 151, 153
Bryk Place 81
'buildings at risk' 13, 14, 61, 77, 121,
   125, 129, 131, 141, 149
Bureau d'Etudes Techniques **114-6**
Burton, Esmond 98
Butler Hegarty Architects 73, 143
buttresses 54, 57-8, 73

C

Cadogan, Edward 98-9
Calvert Avenue 125
campaigns 13, 15, 68, 79, 80, 83, 91,
   105, 130, 140, 144
canals 11, 13, 19, 21, 29, 67, 87, 145
Carless, Capel and Leonard 87
castle: 43, 55, 57, 103
   pumping station 57
Castle Climbing Centre, The **55-8**
Cazenove Architects **69**
chapel 11, 61, 69, 71, 123, 124, 147,
   149-50
charity 15, 59, 61, 77, 133, 153,
Chateau de Chambord 49
Chetwyn, Miss 119
Chimes bar 140
Cholera epidemic 57
churches 11, 14, 15, 55, 69, 71, 73-4,
   83, 107, 109, 123, 124, 141, 145, 147,
   149-50, 155-8
cinema 11, 15, 95, 101, 102, 137,
   139-40
City Academies 39
City Construction Company Ltd 67
City of London 21, 49, 74, 81, 87, 89,
   123, 150
Clapton: 59, 61, 74, 93, 140-41
   Cinematograph Theatre **137-40**
   Federation Synagogue 11, **93-5**
   Girls' School 61
   Park United Reformed Church **69**
   Pond 141, 143-4
   Portico **59-61**
   Portico Learning Centre **59**
   Stadium 15, 102
Clarnico Confectioners 13, 87, 145
classical 29, 55, 57, 61, 69, 75, 95, 107,
   123, 137, 141
Cleeve Workshops 11, **125-7**
Clerkenwell 67, 125
climate change 14
Clissold Park 14, 55, 119
club (society) 11, 13, 97-9, 129-31,
   133, 143, 147
club (nightclub) 139-40
Coates, Nigel 25, 27
Coldplay 71
Combined Electricity and Dust
Destruction Undertaking 111
communal 21, 40, 49, 97-8, 133
concrete 29, 31, 47, 49, 80, 99, 116-7,
   119, 136-7, 144, 151, 153
Congress Hall 61
conservation 6, 51, 83, 143
conservation areas 13, 15, 95, 127,
   141, 144, 150
Conservationists 25, 109
Cook Townsend Architects **55**
cottage 54, 105, 107, 109, 135, 145, 147
County of London Plan 31, 135-6
courtyard 11, 19, 21, 23, 24, 46, 61,
   119, 145, 147
Crane, Lionel 81
creative industries 13, 33
Creed, Marin 61
Cross, A G 75, 77
Cross, Alfred W S 111, 113, 129
Cullinan, Dominic **47-9**

D

Dacombe, Terry **71**
Dacres, Guy-Dance 140

Dalston: 14, 27, 150
   Lane 13
   Theatre 15
Department of Health 151
diverse (ethnicity) 41, 43
Dolins, Daniel 131, 133
Doris's Place 11, **22-4**
Dougie's **137-40**
Douglas fir 46
Douglas, Irvine 139-40
Downs Park Road 39
Duckworth, George 137

E

Eames, Charles and Ray 23, 45
East Cross Route 13, 97
East End 15, 24, 77, 87, 91, 93, 101,
   109, 127, 159
East London 13, 68, 81, 147, 153
   Line 27, 91
Eastern Counties Railway Company 89
Eastway 97, 145, 147
education 11, 14, 31, 39, 43, 61, 65,
   80, 95, 117, 119, 151
Edwardian 75
   Baroque 129
egoism 63
Elizabeth Fry Refuge **133**
energy 14-5, 46, 49, 65
energy efficient 14-5, 21, 37
English Heritage 14-5, 51, 61, 71, 77,
   121, 124, 130-1, 141, 150
English Partnerships 19
entertainment 11, 75, 101, 113
Entwistle, Janet 130
Eton (Etonians) 97, 99, 147
Eton Manor Boys' Club 11, 13, **96-9**
Eton Mission 11, 98, 145, 158
exhibitions 34, 58, 77, 117, 119
experimental 24, 31 65, 116, 127

F

Federation of Synagogues 93
Fellows Court 107, 109
Festival of Britain 117, 119
filter beds 55, 57, 67, 79
First World War 67, 83, 95, 97, 99, 150
FLACQ Architects **44-6**
flats 11, 19, 23-4, 37, 55, 71, 83, 109,
   116, 135-6, 144, 147
Flemish style 113
fly-wheels 57-8
folly 57, 61, 116
Forshaw, John Henry 117, 136
Foster and Partners 41, 43, 91
Free Form Arts Trust 33-4
Fry, Elizabeth 133
Fuller, Henry **69**
functional 35, 55, 61, 77, 102
furniture 21, 41, 53-4, 77, 127

G

Gainsborough Road 88, 97
gallery 11, 24, 27, 33-4, 41, 43, 58, 95,
   119
Gargano, Nicky 99
gas:
   house 55
   plants 13, 19
Gay, Doug 71
Gazette 68, 73, 137, 139, 150
Geffrye Museum 27
Geffrye Museum extension **25-7**

George Wragge Ltd 129
Georgian 11, 141, 143
    neo 21
Gilbert, Anthony 119
Gillum, Mayor William 53-4
Gillum's Fields 54
glass 33-4, 46, 49, 54, 65, 74, 80, 91,
    102, 124, 143
Glass, Marcus **93-5**
Goldfinger, Ernö **29-31**
Goodhart-Rendel, Harry **96-9**
Gordon, Alexander **103-5**
Gothic 11, 54, 69, 124
    Revival 54, 124
Grace, Fred 99
Great Eastern Railway (GER) 89, 91
Greater London Council (GLC) 115
Greek 59, 61, 63, 87, 98, 143
    Doric 59, 61
Green Lanes 55, 79
    Pumping Station **57**
Green, Arthur George 88
greyhound racing 101-2
gymnasium 29, 91, 95, 98-9, 119

H
Hackney:
    Borough Council 67
    Council 13-4, 37, 71, 73, 80, 124,
        127, 130-1, 144, 151
    Downs 40
    Gazette 68, 73, 139
    Historic Buildings Trust 71, 73
    Marshes 67, 115
    Road 107, 109
    Society Design Awards 13
    Volunteers' Social Club 143
    Wick 11, 13, 87-8, 97, 99, 101-2, 115,
        145, 147
Hackney Empire 2-3, 11, 13, 50, **63-5**,
    71
Hackney Stadium **100-2**
Haggerston: 13, 31, 53, 107, 111, 130
    Basin 21
    Swimming Club 130
Haggerston Baths 11, 13, 68, **128-30**
Haggerston School for Girls 11,
    29-31
Harbour, Ivan **47-9**
Hare, Cecil **147**
Hare, H A **113**
Heritage Lottery Fund 14, 27, 61, 65, 77
Heron, Sir John **74**
Hicks, Miss Agnes 68
high-density 14, 21, 91
Holmes, Charlie 80
Homerton High Street 81
Hope Chemical Works 87
Hosking, William **122-4**
hospitals 11, 103, 105
Hothouse **32-4**
housing: 11, 13-5, 19, 21, 24, 35, 37,
    45, 53, 87, 102, 107, 109, 119, 125,
    135-6, 145, 147
    affordable 13, 19, 21, 24, 46
Hoxton 13-5, 21, 53, 107, 109
Hunt, William G **75**
hygiene 111, 113

I
In-Between 11, **35-7**
indoor climbing wall 58
industrial 11, 13, 19, 21, 37, 53-4, 57-8,
    65, 77, 85, 87, 97, 101, 129, 136, 145
industry 13, 27, 77, 87, 88, 127, 145

Inman, William Southcote **59-61**
Institute of International Visual Arts
    (Iniva) 41
iron church 147, 149-50
Islamic 63, 95
Italianate 89, 91

J
Jacobs, Jane 11
Japanese architecture 45
Jay, John 124
Jeffree, Sydney 81
Jekyll, Gertrude 99
Jewish 11, 93, 95, 119
John Scott Health Centre 119

K
Kayaking 80
Kemp, William 67
Kenning Hall Cinema **139**
Kentish ragstone 74
Killby and Gayford 77
Kingsland Road 25, 147
Knights Templar 74

L
Laburnum Street Party 130
Langley, Alfred 89, 91
Le Corbusier 24, 109, 136, 151
Lea Bridge Road 93, 156
Learning Trust 61
Lee Navigation Canal 21, 87, 141, 145
Lee, Marcus 45
Leonardo da Vinci 49
Lewis, C W 119
library 14, 31, 41, 43, 67, 98, 111, 113
linenfold panelling 81, 83
Linscott Road 59, 61
Little, George Herbert 125
Liverpool Street station 91
live-work 11, 53
local protest 57
Loddiges, George 33, 124, 161
Loggia 65, 130
London Borough of Hackney (LBH)
    13-4, 61, 127
LBH Parks Department 144
LBH Training Centre for Adults with
Learning Disabilities **151**
London County Council (LCC) 27, 31,
    67, 109, 117, 119, 125, 127, 135-6, 151
    LCC Architects' Department 31,
    117, 127, 135-6, 151
    LCC Parks Department 67
    LCC Schools Division 117
London Development Agency (LDA)
    102
London Fields: 14, 23, 33-4, 67-8
    User Group 68
London Fields Lido 11, 14, **66-8**
London Orphan Asylum **59-61**
London Water Ring Main 79
Long, Cesar A 75
Lost Hackney 85, 109
Loudon, John 123
Lower Clapton Road 59, 69, 103, 105,
    137, 139, 141, 143
Lubetkin, Berthold 21

M
Mackintosh, Dr Donald **105**
Malin, Harry 99
Manor Garden Allotments 99
manufactories 53, 127
Mapledene Pubic Inquiry 13

Mare Street 63, 65, 73, 131
Marks Barfield Architects **79-80**
Marshall, Sir Chapman 123
Matcham, Frank 3, **63-5**
mayors 68, 77, 123, 129, 137
Mayor of Hackney 68, 137
Medieval 11, 14, 57-8, 73-4
Mental Health Act 151
Metropolitan Asylum Boards 61
Metropolitan Borough of Shoreditch
    77, 111, 113, 130
Metropolitan Water Act 57, 79
Minton-Taylor, Reginald **125-7**
missionary 103, 147
Modernism 23, 117, 135-6
Modernist 11, 29, 35, 79, 119, 139
Morning Lane 69, 151, 153
Morris, William 11, 53, 153
Mossbourne Community Academy
    11, 39-40, 47
Mothers' Hospital, The **103-5**
Mothers' Square 103, 105
municipal 75, 77, 111, 113, 127, 130
Murray Grove 21
museum 11, 25, 27, 83, 88, 111, 124
Museum of London 159-60
music 13, 27, 40, 65, 71, 139-40
Myddleton, Sir Hugh 79
Mylne, William Chadwell **55-7**, 79

N
Narroway, The 73
National Health Service (NHS) 41,
    103, 105
National Lottery 15, 27, 80
National Trust 81, 83
nature reserve 79
Needwood House 135-6
Neoclassical 61, 143
Neo-Corbusian 24
New Lansdowne Club **131-3**
New River 79, 136
New River Company 55, 57, 79
Niall Phillips Architects **75**
Nicholas Grimshaw and Partners **55**
Nicholl House 15, **134-6**
Nichols Square **107-9**
Nichols, John 107
Nichols, Richard 107
Nonconformist 59, 69, 124, 149
North London Railway 145
Northaird Point 14-5, **114-6**

O
Oasis 71
Old Nichol 127, 162
Old Street 75, 111
Olympic 13, 99, 102, 145, 147
open-air swimming 67
Orientalism 95
orphanage 61
Oxbridge 97, 145, 147

P
Palace Pavilion 11, 15, **137-40**
Palladio 49, 153
panelling 29, 31, 39, 81. 83, 119
Parkesine 87
Parks and Open Spaces Committee
    68
Peabody Trust, The 21
Peerless Pool 67
Perpendicular 35, 74, 147
Peter Barber Architects 12, **22-4**
Pevsner, Nickolaus 51, 54, 68, 93, 109

photovoltaic cells 34
Pinter, Harold 39
Pitfield Street 111, 113
Pitfield Street Baths and Washhouses 11, 111, 113, **128-30**
planar 31
planning 11,13-5, 24, 37, 46, 54, 102, 135
Pond House **141-4**
post-war 13, 15, 31, 116, 119, 135-6
Powys, Albert 73
prefabricated 21, 45, 117
Pre-Raphaelite 54
Princess Louise 103, 105
pubic housing 136
public baths 111, 113, 129
public health 54, 111, 129
pumping stations 55, 57-8
purpose-built 11, 53, 59, 93, 125

Q
Queen Victoria 59, 103, 105
Queensbridge Road 19, 21, 29

R
radical 11, 35, 133, 135
railway 11, 27, 33-4, 40 75, 87, 89, 91, 109, 145
Raines Court 21
rational 31, 91
recycled 37, 46-7
Red House 53
Reed, Dr Andrew 61
regeneration 14, 21, 24, 33, 102
Regent's Canal 13, 19
religious 11, 14, 69, 103, 123, 133
reservoirs 55, 79-80, 136
residential 19, 37, 45, 57, 59, 116, 127
Reynolds, Fiona 83
Richard Griffiths Architects **81-3**
Richard Rogers Partnership 39, 47
Riches Ullmayer and Gariboldo **35-7**
Richmond Road 33
Riseholme Street 97-8
River Lea 15, 87, 99, 143
River Thames 87
Rivington Place **41-3**
Robertson Davies, William 63
Robinson, Elizabeth 11-2, 14, 25, 85, 145
Rogers Stirk Harbour and Partners **39-40**
Rogers, Dr Nathaniel 124
Romanesque 69
Ronalds, Tim 9, 12, 14, 33, **63-5**
Round Chapel, The **69-71**
Rowbotham, H A **66-8**
Rowe Lane 11, **44-6**

S
S&P Architects **66-8**
Sadleir, Ralph **81**
Salvation Army 61, 103, 105
Samuely, Felix 117
Save Sutton House Campaign 83
Save the Reservoirs Campaign 79-80
school 11, 15, 29, 31, 39-40, 59, 61, 69, 71, 81, 83, 88, 93, 97, 117, 119, 130, 147, 150-1
Scottish Baronial style 57
sculpture 29, 65, 119
Seagal, Walter 45
Second World War 68, 83, 93, 99, 102-3, 113, 130, 139
Sedgemore, Brian 116

self-build 35, 45, 47
Shakespeare 54
shopfronts 23, 53-4
Shoreditch: 11-45, 21, 23, 41, 53, 75, 77, 87, 89, 91, 107, 109, 111, 113, 127, 129-30
High Street 89
Town Hall 11, 75, 77
Vestry 111, 113
Siberian larch 19, 45
Sight of Eternal Life Church **148-50**
slipper baths 111, 113, 129
slum clearance 135
slums 14, 21, 24, 116, 127, 135
Smithson, T L **66-8**
social 11, 13, 15, 19, 21, 24, 31, 39-40, 43, 58, 71, 97, 103, 109, 116-7, 127, 133, 143-5, 153
social housing 21, 153
Socialism 53
socially progressive 53, 117
Society for the Preservation of Ancient Buildings (SPAB) 73
solar 46
Space Studios 120, **151-3**
Spalding, Henry **110-3**
speculators 53
speedway 101-2
Spitalfields 91
sport 40, 68, 80, 98, 130, 139, 145
square 19
St Augustine's Tower **72-4**
St John Institute 83
St John-at-Hackney Church 73
St Mary of Eton Church 97, **145-7**
stadium 15, 99, 101-2
stained glass 124
Stamford Hill 11, 55, 95
steam 57, 89, 91, 111
Stirling Castle 57
Stirling Prize 41
Stoke Newington 15, 21, 37, 55, 71, 74, 79, 124, 136
Stoke Newington West Reservoir Centre 79
markets 11, 14, 102
Street, George Edmund 54
Stuart Hall Library 41
stucco 61, 81, 109, 141, 144
Sugar, Sir Alan 65
sustainability 15, 19, 21, 37, 40, 45-6
Sutton House 71, **81-3**, 131
swimming pools 14, 67-8, 113, 129-30

T
tailor 95, 127
Tall Buildings Strategy 14
Tanhouse 81, 83
Tassell, Wally 130
Taylor, John Henry **106-9**
Temperance Movement 54, 133, 150
tenements 54, 74
terraces 11. 13, 15, 29, 33-5, 37, 40, 53-4, 65, 68, 107, 109, 130, 141, 145
terracotta 65, 80, 91
Thames Water 79-80
The Deptford Trilogy 63
The London Plan 14
theatres 11, 15, 41, 51, 63, 65, 137, 139-40
Thomas Sutton 81, 83
Tim Ronalds Architects 14, **62-5**
timber 13, 15, 19, 21, 29, 31, 37, 45-6, 49, 54, 119, 144, 151

timber-framed 35, 37, 39-40, 43, 45, 150
tower blocks 11, 13, 21, 116
Tower Hamlets 127
town hall 11-2, 57, 57, 65, 74-5, 77
trade union 83
transport 11, 13-4, 21, 39, 83, 91
Trowbridge Estate 15, **114-6**
Truman's Road **47-9**
Tudor Gothic 107, 109
Tupper and Company, Messrs **148-50**
Tuscan 61, 109
typhoid epidemic 61

U
unmarried 103, 105
Urswick, Christopher **74**

V
vestry 75, 77 111, 113
viaduct 33-4, 75, 89, 91
Victorian 13-4, 23, 35, 37, 53-4, 57-8, 61, 63, 65, 71, 75, 95, 105, 111, 113, 124, 143, 147, 149
Victorian terraces 13, 35
villas 95, 133, 141
Villiers, Arthur 98-9

W
W&C French **78-80**
Wagg, Alfred 97-8
Wakeling, B J 129
Walker, Cyril 136
War Damage Committee 113
warehouse 13, 21, 88, 91, 101
Waterden Road 101
Webb, Philip 11, **52-4**
Wellesley, Gerald 97-8
Wenlock Barn 81, 83
Weymouth Terrace 29
Whatcott's Yard 35, 37
Whitechapel 93
wholesalers 53, 127
Wilderness, The 99
Willersley Castle 103, 105
Williams-Samuels, Barrington 140
Wilshaw, Sir Michael 40
women 95, 97, 103, 105, 111, 113, 129, 133, 139
Wood, Richard 21
Wood, Sancton 89
Woodberry Down: 15, 117, 119, 124, 135-6, 156, 161, 165
Woodberry Down Comprehensive School 15, 84, **117-9**
Estate 117, 119, 135
Primary School 119
woodland burial gardens 123
woodworking 127
Working Men's Club 133, 147
workshop 11, 43, 53-4, 57, 83, 95, 119, 125, 127, 153
workspaces 33-4
Worship Street 11, **52-4**
Wright, Carel 119
wrought iron 54, 88, 141, 143